WERE YOU BORN
FOR EACH OTHER?

WERE YOU BORN FOR EACH OTHER?

Finding, Catching, and Keeping the Love of Your Life

DR. KEVIN LEMAN

**Delacorte
Press**

Published by
Delacorte Press
Bantam Doubleday Dell Publishing Group, Inc.
666 Fifth Avenue
New York, New York 10103

Library of Congress Cataloging-in-Publication Data

Leman, Kevin.
Were you born for each other? : finding, catching, and keeping the love of your life / Kevin Leman.
p.   cm.
Includes bibliographical references and index.
ISBN 0-385-29923-0 (hc)
1. Mate selection.   2. Marriage—Psychological aspects.   3. Love—Psychological aspects.   4. Birth order—Psychological aspects.
I. Title.
HQ801.L383   1991   90-38205
646.7′7—dc20   CIP

Manufactured in the United States of America
Published simultaneously in Canada

February 1991

10 9 8 7 6 5 4 3 2 1
RRH

To our friends—

Tom and Wendy Dietsch,
Mike and Sandy Smith,
Bill and Laverne Foster,
and Joe and Teri Robinette.

You really were born for each other!

Love,
Cub and Sande

CONTENTS

Part Five
. . . And the Greatest Is Love

PART ONE

About This Thing Called Birth Order

1

Taking a Tour of the Family Zoo

So you've got romance on your mind?

Maybe you've got stars in your eyes. Or perhaps you're looking for someone who'll put some stars in your eyes.

Whichever is the case, if you're interested in l-o-v-e, then this book is for you!

I don't know what state your love life is in, but whatever it is, this book is for you. It could be that:

—You've just seen the person you think might be Mr. or Ms. Right, but you want to know how you can be sure.

—You found Mr. Right a long time ago, but you've been married to him for so long that the shine on that golden boy has turned a bit green. Now you're wondering what you can do to bring that old sparkle back into your relationship.

—There's no one special in your life right now, but you'd really like to find him or her. You're just not sure the best way to go about it.

—You're dating someone, and it seems to be getting serious, but you'd like to be sure you're headed in the right direction. You can't decide whether you ought to be moving "full speed ahead" or if it's time to slam that gearshift into reverse and head in the opposite direction.

Stay tuned, if any of these descriptions fit you, because I'm going to turn you into a first-class Romantic Detective.

Before we're through, you'll be able to out-Columbo Peter Falk, outdeduce Sherlock Holmes, and make *Murder, She Wrote*'s Jessica Fletcher look like a bumbler! At least when it comes to love and marriage.

What that means is that I'll help you decide what you need to be looking for in a partner. I'll help you figure out if the person you're dating is the person you ought to be dating. I'll tell you how to keep from being "blinded" by love and help you to predict the problems that might lie ahead.

If you're married and the excitement of romance has been replaced by the dullness of routine, I'll tell you some things you can do to rediscover the thrill you used to know. I'll also give you some insights into your spouse's personality (and your own personality too) that will help you to nurture, and perhaps even save, your marriage.

And none of this will have anything to do with whether your horoscopes are compatible, your karmas match, or anything else of the sort. Rather, it has to do with birth order.

Birth order? you ask. What's that?

Put simply, birth order has to do with where you fit into your family, which in turn has a great deal to do with who you are. Furthermore, being able to pick up the clues from others so you know how their birth orders have shaped them will give you a great advantage in the romantic arena.

For instance, suppose Sally Ann, who is nineteen, the youngest girl in a family of four children, is at a party.

There are three guys there who seem interested and interesting, and she wouldn't mind going out with any of them.

There's Tom, who's impeccably dressed, without a hair out of place, the epitome of grace and charm.

And Bill, the fun-loving sort. He's laid back, the life of the party, and his carefree attitude is in total contrast to Tom's "perfect" behavior.

And Roger, who doesn't seem to have Tom's grace or Bill's fun-loving attitude, but who is a nice, friendly guy.

Now, there's no way Sally Ann can get to know these men in anything other than a superficial way on her first meeting.

But if she is a Romantic Detective she'll have a better chance of figuring out which one of these fellows is most deserving of her telephone number.

Or consider Megan and Bryan. They've been dating for a couple of months, and the future is looking bright.

They think they're in love, but then one night they arrive at the theater to see a movie Bryan is really interested in, only to find that it's sold out. Bryan throws an absolute fit, and Megan is shocked and disgusted. She realizes for the first time that she really doesn't know him all that well.

What could she have done to get to know him better?

Does Bryan's emotional outburst necessarily mean that Megan needs to end the relationship?

And how does any dating couple know whether the time has come to abandon the relationship and begin looking elsewhere for Mr. or Ms. Right?

And then there's the married couple that has come to act like Mr. and Mrs. Wrong. I've seen these couples dozens of times in my private practice in Tucson.

They sit in my office, smoldering with anger.

I can see it burning in their eyes. Each one of them has "had it up to here" with the other's attitude, and both of them are just about ready to let their marriage take its place in the history books. (But then, of course, they're both still holding on at the same time, or they wouldn't have come to see me.)

Each one of them has a list of complaints a mile or more long, and neither one of them sees how he could possibly be the least little bit at fault.

She's driving him crazy because she doesn't have a spontaneous bone in her body—even when it comes to sex. If he takes one step outside of the routine it throws her into a spin and she doesn't know what to do.

She's upset with him because he just won't seem to stand up for himself. He lets people walk all over him and if there's something he can put off doing, you can bet he will. He's the world champion procrastinator—except when it comes to sex, and then he's always ready!

That's just the tip of the iceberg. The list goes on and on, but the gist of the matter is that they don't see eye to eye on very much of anything.

What happened to this once-loving couple? Is there any chance for their marriage? Why are they so different in their approaches to life?

Let me take those questions one at a time:

Question Number One: What happened to this couple is that their birth orders caught up with them. When they were "falling in love," they didn't notice the character traits in each other that they find so aggravating now. Because of their respective birth orders, they were not ideally suited for each other. More about that later.

Question Number Two: Is there hope for this couple? Absolutely. Well, probably. Okay . . . maybe. They have to work at understanding why they behave as they do, and then work to change the behavior that so irritates the other partner.

Question Number Three: Their approaches to life are different primarily because birth order—where you were born into your family—is one of the primary factors that shapes your approach to life.

Ignoring Birth Order Can Be Bad for You!

More and more these days, churches and synagogues are asking prospective married couples to undergo premarital counseling. I'm all in favor of this. I believe it's a marvelous idea, and one that is sure to spare much in the way of difficulties a few years, months, or perhaps even weeks, down the road.

Too many men and women stand at the altar together without knowing anything about each other. They know they're in love with "the most wonderful person in the world." But they don't know what that "most wonderful" person's likes and dislikes are. During the courtship, in fact, both of these "wonderful" folks have been working as hard as possible to smother each other in sweetness and light, and it's possible that neither one of them has even allowed the other to catch a glimpse of the person beneath the smiling mask.

How many times, I wonder, has a husband or wife said, "Whatever happened to that sweet person I married?" The answer is that this person never really even existed! I would even be willing to bet that Cinderella discovered a few annoying traits in Prince Charming's personality once she moved into the palace. For instance, the polite charm that had so captivated the young beauty no doubt started to seem condescending and chauvinistic after a while. And to make matters worse, the prince rarely remembered to put the toilet seat down.

So, insofar as the premarital counseling is designed to help eliminate unpleasant surprises and open starry eyes about what it really takes to live with someone day after day and year after year, I'm all for it.

But at the same time it bothers me that such counseling rarely takes birth order into account—and birth order is an extremely important factor in achieving marital happiness.

By giving you a better understanding of birth order and how it relates to love and marriage, this book will help anyone who is contemplating marriage, wants to improve a marriage, or is looking for a lifetime partner. Coming up, we'll tell you:

—which birth order is most compatible with yours

—which birth order is most likely to clash with yours

—what sorts of questions you should be asking to determine if that special person is really right for you

—what you can do to overcome birth-order differences

—how to see the roadblocks to marital happiness that may lie ahead

However, before we can delve into birth order's influence in romance and marriage, it's important to get an understanding of the various birth-order positions within the family.

What Is Birth Order?

Often when I'm speaking at seminars or appearing on talk shows I'm asked how I got interested in birth order.

Well, it all happened in 1967, my first year in graduate school at the University of Arizona. I was introduced to the subject by the internationally known psychologist Dr. Oscar Christensen, who fascinated me with his description of the way the various members of a family could be expected to behave. As I heard him talk about birth-order differences I knew that his theories fit my family perfectly.

Dr. Christensen didn't originate the idea of birth order. The pioneering psychologist Alfred Adler was the first to see a correlation between where a person was born into a family and that person's approach to life. He conducted extensive studies that showed that birth order is a significant factor in personality development, behavior, and outlook.

In my years as a practicing psychologist I have seen Adler's theories supported again and again.

There are actually three major birth orders: Firstborn, Middle Child, and Last Born. There is one other birth position that might be considered separate and apart from the others, and this is the Only Child. Actually, though, the Only Child usually takes on all the characteristics of the Firstborn—and then some. For this reason the Only Child is sometimes considered to be a "Super First-born."

It is a scientific fact, proven time and again, that your position in your family shapes your approach to life.

Before we talk about how birth orders match or don't match in romantic situations, I want to take you on a brief tour of the birth orders themselves, with a look at some of the strengths and weaknesses of each.

Only Child

The Only Child, otherwise known as the Super Firstborn, has been the recipient of a bum rap over the years. Only Children are supposed to be selfish and spoiled. They supposedly breeze through life without giving a single thought to the welfare of others.

This may be true in some instances, but it is certainly far from a general rule, and to put all Only Children into this category is to do them a disservice.

For one thing, there are a number of reasons why someone may be an Only Child, and each of these reasons would have a bearing on the way his parents treated him. If, for example, Little Egbert's mom and dad wanted to have more children but couldn't, for whatever reason, then they are more likely to treat him as a special little jewel, spoil him rotten, and wind up with an adult son who always has to wrestle with his own selfishness. If, on the other hand, they never wanted children in the first place, and always viewed little Eggie as something of an unfortunate accident, then he's just as likely to grow up in an atmosphere of emotional indifference—and that will do anything but spoil him.

It could be true, too, that his parents would like to have had more children, but didn't feel they could afford more than one. If this is the case, it's highly unlikely that they're going to be buying Gerber's brand of caviar for him when he's an infant. In other words, rich parents are likely to give their children many things, no matter how many children they may have. Less well-off parents will not be able to spoil their children by inundating them with material possessions, even if they have only one child.

So much for the myth about Only Children. But what is the reality?

Most of the Only Children I've worked with are nice, responsible people. As for his best personality traits, the Only Child tends to be extremely reliable and conscientious. If you want something done and you want it done right, he's a good person to give the assignment to. In addition he tends to be intellectual, studious, and quite serious.

Have you ever seen a Ted Koppel interview? When you see him you're seeing an Only Child at work. Personally, I love the guy. He interviews with the precision and skill of a surgeon. He can absolutely take a guest apart. And then, just before time expires he's able to sum up, sew up, and capsulize the entire program. In my opinion he's the best interviewer around.

There are other Only Children who are excellent interviewers as well: I think of Arsenio Hall, J. P. McCarthy at WJR radio in Detroit, and Pat McMahon of KTAR in Phoenix.

You'll often find that the Only Child is superconservative by nature inasmuch as he has usually spent more time with Mom and Dad than do children with siblings, who spend time with their brothers and sisters. Because he has spent so much time with people who are older, he has more than likely acted like a "little adult" most of his life and has accepted his parents' views of life as his own.

When I say he's conservative, I want you to understand that I mean he is likely to be the one who carries on the family tradition and upholds the beliefs of his mom and dad. But if Ma and Pa happened to be a couple of Bohemian artists living in Greenwich Village, don't expect their offspring to be wearing a three-piece suit and carrying a briefcase. *Conservative* in this case would mean that he'd hold to tradition and do his best to be a nonconformist.

Some of the negative traits that are often associated with Only Children are that they may be perfectionistic and critical. It is not

FIRSTBORN

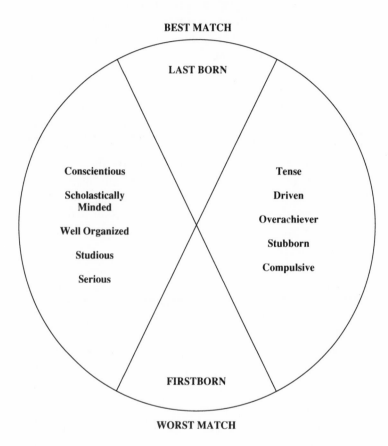

BEST MATCH

LAST BORN

Conscientious

Scholastically Minded

Well Organized

Studious

Serious

Tense

Driven

Overachiever

Stubborn

Compulsive

FIRSTBORN

WORST MATCH

unusual to find that they are more critical of themselves than they are of others. This is due to the fact that they have spent their childhood years trying to live up to their parents' expectations. Many Only Children have a tendency to believe that whatever they do is never quite good enough. I call these people "discouraged perfectionists" and their ranks are made up almost entirely of Only Children and Firstborns.

Another problem for the Only Child is that sharing has never been a major issue in his life. He didn't have to share his toys, his room, or his clothes. It's not that he's self-absorbed and greedy, just that he never had to share with others.

An Only Child acquaintance of mine, who is about to be married, recently confided in me that "the thought of having to think about someone else scares me half to death."

I said before that I often refer to Only Children as Super Firstborns, because they have all the traits of Firstborns carried to the utmost degree. While that's true, Only Children differ in that they can demonstrate the tendencies of both Firstborn and Last-Born children (which in some cases is a mixture that makes Jekyll-Hyde seem like a normal guy). This is because that's really what they are—Firstborn and Last Born rolled into one.

If Only Children don't develop into supercritical types, then they are likely to become "rescuers," people who are always rushing to the aid of those in need. This makes for troubling relationships, especially in the area of romance, because a rescuer is likely to mistake sympathy for love and develop emotional attachments to those who are in need of a helping hand. Being interested in helping people is certainly a noble characteristic—but the rescuer takes this interest to ridiculous extremes, with the result that he unintentionally hurts someone, or lets someone take advantage of him.

If you're an Only Child you're keeping company with the likes of Ted Koppel, Steve Allen, Lauren Bacall, Dick Cavett, Franklin D. Roosevelt, Charles Lindbergh, Leonardo da Vinci, T. Boone Pickens, Carl Icahn, and Joe Montana.

Firstborns

Psychologist Lucille Forer said that Firstborns "tend to be more conscientious, achieve higher scholastically, and go to school longer than later-borns. They also are more apt to become scientists or eminent in their chosen careers than are later children in the family." But she also said the Firstborn "may be tense and driven" and noted that parents, "also expect a higher level of achievement from their first child than from later children."[1]

These words have been verified many times by independent research. What do Firstborns do when they grow up? They may become astronauts or get elected to Congress. Or it's possible that they will be talk-show hosts. Firstborns are highly represented in each of these high-profile professions.

It is also true that a much higher proportion of doctors, engineers, and attorneys are Firstborns than one would expect based on the percentage of Firstborns in the general population.

The Firstborn is likely to be very well organized, studious, and serious. He's the type of person whom those of us who might be just a teensy-weensy bit jealous would call an overachiever. As a general rule he likes being in control of things, and he doesn't like surprises. He is likely to be quite comfortable in an existence that other birth orders would find monotonous or routine.

The Firstborn is used to being a big deal, and he's not afraid when and if he finds himself in the spotlight. After all, when he was a child, everything he did was cause for jubilation.

"Look, honey! Mary Elizabeth is about to take her first step!"

"Oh, wow! Really? Where's the video camera? Where's the video camera?"

But a couple of kids later, little Herkimer is about to take his first steps, and do you think anyone is paying attention? No way. They're too busy watching Mary Elizabeth, who has just learned how to whistle.

You see, whatever the Firstborn does for the first time is a very big event. But by the time the second, third, and subsequent children do it, it's no big deal because everybody's seen it before!

I can see the letters already: "Dear Dr. Leman, I'll have you know we've prided ourselves on giving just as much attention to our sons Harlan and Buford as we do to our Firstborn, Festus, Jr."

Well, if you've done that, congratulations to you, because you've done something very few parents manage to do.

MIDDLE BORN

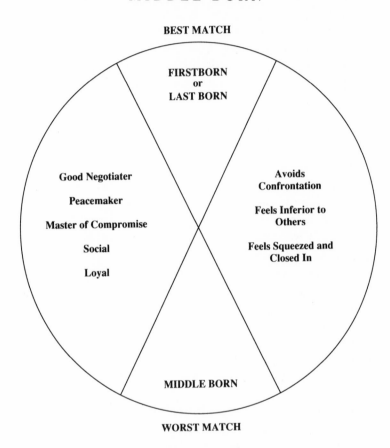

Now, for the Firstborn there is a down side to all this attention, in that he is expected to do everything better than the other children. Not only that, but he's expected to be a role model for his brothers and sisters, and that means that his failures and short-comings are magnified every bit as much as his accomplishments. The Firstborn is also expected to help keep the other kids in line.

Ask a Firstborn what he remembers best about his childhood

and he's likely to say, "What childhood?" He's not being flippant, either, because he was always expected to be the little adult. Because of this, some Firstborns wait until they're in their late thirties or early forties, decide they want to find out what they've missed, and have a childhood then. And, of course, that creates problems for all concerned—especially husbands or wives.

Usually, Firstborns will develop in one of two directions:

1. They will be compliant people who seek to please everyone else.
2. They will be hard-driving, aggressive types whose one goal in life is to climb to the top.

The compliant Firstborn is the model child who never gives his parents a moment of grief. He thrives on their approval, and later on in life he thrives on the approval of his boss, his co-workers, and his spouse. This person's intentions are good—he wants to make people happy—but the problem is that there are always a few less-than-noble souls around who are ready to take advantage of his tendency to please.

The strong-willed type of Firstborn is the one who was always urged by his parents to "do the best," "be the best," and so on. He's never learned that you don't always have to be number one, and that it is okay sometimes just to know you worked as hard as you could.

He is likely to be a workaholic who can hardly stand to sit idly for a moment. Sooner or later, though, he pays the price for his life-style. He destroys his health, ruins his relationships with his family, or both.

When you consider the innate drive of the Firstborn, it's no surprise that several American presidents were the first children in their families, including Harry Truman, Lyndon Johnson, and Jimmy Carter. Other famous Firstborns include Alexander Hamilton, Henry Ford, Katharine Hepburn, Gloria Steinem, Pablo Picasso, and Norman Mailer.

Numerous TV personalities, and especially talk-show hosts, are either Firstborns or Only Children, including Phil Donahue,

Oprah Winfrey, Sonya Friedman, Geraldo Rivera, Arsenio Hall, and Sally Jessy Raphael. On a recent thirty-one-city tour, I was interviewed by some ninety-two talk-show hosts, and only five of these were not Firstborns or Onlies.

Middle Children

Have you got a secret that's just too good to keep to yourself? You want to tell someone, but it has to be someone you can trust. Who can you tell? Well, I wouldn't advise you to go around telling secrets to anyone, but if you have to tell somebody, take it from me and tell a Middle Child.

Middle Children are the most secretive of the birth orders. They're noted for playing it "close to the vest" and for being rather wary about divulging their true feelings and motivations. Thus they are generally good keepers of secrets.

Part of the reason for this may be their position in the middle. They hear the secrets of their Firstborn sibling, as well as the secrets of the Last Born.

Their position in the middle also helps these people develop into good negotiaters. They tend to be peacemakers, masters of compromise, sometimes even at their own expense. They will tend to run from any sort of confrontation, even when confrontation is necessary.

The personality of the Middle Child is the most mysterious and hard to figure of all the birth orders. There are so many variables pushing and pulling the poor Middle Child that it is not always so easy to determine how he's going to turn out.

The most obvious observation I can make about this person is that when he was growing up he was always caught in the middle. He was born too late to get the privileges and perks that go to the Firstborn, and he was born too soon to get the freedom that often goes to the Last Born when the parents relax the disciplinary reins. He's stuck somewhere between his birthstone and a hard place.

The Middle Born's personality depends a great deal on his older

LAST BORN

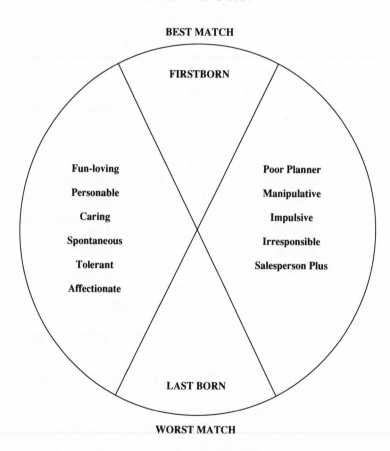

BEST MATCH

FIRSTBORN

Fun-loving	Poor Planner
Personable	Manipulative
Caring	Impulsive
Spontaneous	Irresponsible
Tolerant	Salesperson Plus
Affectionate	

LAST BORN

WORST MATCH

brother(s) or sister(s). He may decide to compete with the First-born in every area, but if the competition is too stiff, he's just as likely to go off in the opposite direction.

For instance, if Firstborn is a borderline genius who never gets anything less than an A in school, her little sister may know it's useless for her to try to compete. As a result she may show no interest at all in academics and instead throw her energies into sports.

On the other hand, if big sister is a beauty who is admired by the boys in seven western states, the Middle Born may throw herself into academics with a passion, realizing that this is the way she'll get some recognition for herself. What I'm saying is that if you want to understand the Middle Child, you need to take a good look at the Firstborn. The second child always plays off the first, especially when there are fewer than five years separating the two.

A problem for many Middle Borns is that they tend to feel anonymous. They were always a part of the family, but they never felt that there was anything special about them. Eventually most of them come to relish this sort of anonymity, and they are content to live their lives far from the spotlight. Again, this is not a universal truth, and you will find some Middle Borns, such as John F. Kennedy, Richard Nixon, Michael J. Fox, and Barbara Walters, who have enjoyed life in the public eye.

One thing I can say with near certainty is that a Middle Born is likely to have more friends than his Firstborn and Lastborn siblings. Middle Borns tend to make friends easily and they have many of them. During their teen years Middle Borns are more likely to "run with the pack" as they seek to obtain from their friends what they think they've missed from their families. At home Buford isn't anything special, but his friends treat him like a king.

Unfortunately Buford's friends may not be worth a pound and a half of chopped liver, but you'll never convince him of that fact! He thinks they'd do anything for him, and he'll do anything for them. There's been more than one Middle Born who's gotten himself into trouble with that kind of thinking.

Later in life the Middle Born will still have lots of friends, and these relationships will be relatively stable. Speaking of stable relationships, Middle Borns have the best record when it comes to lasting marriages. This is the most monogamous birth order.

When you think of Hollywood marriages, what kind of image comes to mind? His fifth and her sixth? "Married in Las Vegas Saturday according to their press agents"?

Well, in contrast think of the marriages of men like Bob Hope and George Burns, both of whom are Middle Borns. George Burns still talks of Gracie reverently and passionately, even though she died in 1964. A Middle Born is likely to be a "one-woman man" or a "one-man woman."

Actually, being a Middle Born is not half bad. Middle Borns have fewer hangups than Firstborns or Last Borns, which is another way of saying this is the most balanced birth-order group. They're generally better adjusted and can cope more effectively with some of life's unpleasant moments.

There is a problem here, though, because Middle Borns are disappearing from the American landscape. The average family these days consists of 1.6 children, and that means we're eliminating the Middle Child. Do that and you eliminate a great many negotiaters, compromisers, and easygoing people who are able to roll with the punches.

You'll also eliminate many of the best entrepreneurs, men like Donald Trump, who says, "I like making deals, preferably big deals, that's how I get my kicks."[2] That is a statement worthy of a Middle Child, and it shows that Donald Trump has made the most of his natural inclination as a Middle Child. CEO's are most likely First Borns who have come up through the ranks, but your entrepreneurs are more likely to come from the middle position.

The Middle Child may be more anonymous than his older and younger siblings, but his anonymity doesn't change the fact that he's an important individual. I hate to think about what the world would be like without him.

If you're a Middle Born, your birth order includes, besides those mentioned earlier, Hubert Humphrey, John Quincy Adams, Susan B. Anthony, Herbert Hoover, Joan Baez, Dwight Eisenhower, Woodrow Wilson, and Benjamin Franklin.

Last Borns

If you're going to throw a party and want everyone to have a good time, you'd be wise to invite several Last Borns. These are the fun-loving, good-time folks. If, on the other hand, you're looking for someone who is always looking ahead and planning seriously for the future, a Last Born may not be the person you want. This birth order is not noted for being forward looking.

Are you a Last Born? If so, is your blood pressure going up as you read this description of you, or has your face broken into a smile of recognition? Before I go any farther, let me tell you that I can be as hard on Last Borns as I want to be. After all, I'm a Last Born myself, and that gives me the right. When it comes to the other birth positions, I know what I'm talking about because of my years in private practice as a psychologist. But when I talk about the Last Born, it's more than that. Not only have I seen it, but I've done it too!

When I was a boy in school, you might have thought my middle name was "Class Clown." If it wasn't Kevin "Class Clown" Leman, it might have been Kevin "Underachiever" Leman. I was in this world to have a good time, pure and simple, and everything else was of secondary importance. You can understand why a Last Born would behave this way when you consider that as the baby he is very often allowed to be "cute" well past the age when his older siblings were expected to "act their age." He is used to being in the family spotlight, and he often finds that he likes it there.

If it sounds to you like I'm being hard on the Last Borns among us, let me remind you of what I said earlier. Every birth position has its bad points, but every position also has its good points. There's nothing wrong with liking a good time or wanting to be the life of the party and make other people laugh. Last Borns know how to enjoy life.

But the Last Born does have a problem when it comes to planning properly for the future. He has always had someone around to take care of him, and he believes it is always going to be that way. Mom and Dad always took special care of him because he was the baby.

For instance, if the Last Born was involved in a fight with his big brother, it didn't matter who started it, Mom was probably going to yell at the older brother and tell him to quit picking on the little guy.

If the Last Born got into any trouble at school, his parents were more likely to come to his rescue because, after all, little Hieronymus just couldn't do anything that naughty. Whatever predicament he got himself into, he knew that Mom and Dad were going to bail him out. As a result he's grown up with the attitude that someone is always going to be there to smooth things out for him and make them better.

If it wasn't Mom and Dad who were looking out for him, it was his big brother, who didn't let the other kids in the neighborhood pick on him, or big sister, who helped him get his homework done on time after he had goofed around all evening.

Because he was treated in these ways when he was a child, it's easy to see why the Last Born can sometimes develop into the Little Prince or Little Princess.

Have you ever heard a woman complain, "My husband didn't really need a wife—he needed a mother"? Chances are, she's married to a Last Born.

But the news isn't all bad. Not by any means. So what are some of the Last Born's good points?

They are personable people, for one thing, and they're generally the kind of people others want to have around. They tend to be genuinely caring people, too, and they're great listeners to other people's problems.

Last Borns often wind up in jobs that are people oriented, such as teaching or counseling. This is not only because they relate well to others, but because they genuinely like other people and want to be around them.

Part of the reason for this, too, is that Last Borns don't get their feathers ruffled as easily as those from the other birth orders. If someone says something hurtful, a serious-minded Firstborn may have his feelings hurt and keep them hurt for quite some time. A freewheeling Last Born, on the other hand, would be more likely to let those words roll off his shoulders. He may be hurt, but he'll get over it sooner, figuring it's all a part of life.

The Last Born tends to have an easy time talking to people and gaining their confidence. (Because this is characteristic of Last Borns, many of them wind up in sales positions.) This is a good trait, unless it crosses the line and becomes an ability to manipulate people and win their confidence undeservedly.

See the guy on TV selling his used cars—banging on the hood and saying, "Ain't she a beaut?" Chances are very good that he's a Last Born. Now, I'm not saying that this car ain't really a beaut. It very well may be. But whatever shape the car's in, a Last Born will do the best job of selling it.

When you think of political conventions, do you remember a particular speech that was outstanding and inspirational? Perhaps your mind may go back to the 1984 Democratic convention when baby-of-the-family Governor Mario Cuomo of New York delivered a speech that will long be remembered by both Democrats and Republicans. Or, I wonder if you may be thinking of the "Great Communicator" himself, Ronald Wilson Reagan—one of only five youngest children ever to occupy the White House. I don't want to become too "political" here—but if communication skills have very much to do with being elected to the presidency, let me be the first to suggest that Mario Cuomo has a legitimate shot at being Last Born number six at the Pennsylvania Avenue address.

Another thing to keep in mind about Last Borns is that they may be filled with ambivalent feelings and uncertainties. They may be charming and engaging one minute, and then rebellious and angry the next. The Last Born may be swinging on a star at nine o'clock and feeling down in the dumps by nine-fifteen.

Why does this happen? Most likely it's due to the way Last Borns are treated when they're children. They're praised and spoiled one minute, and then laughed at and made fun of the next.

For instance, little Gertrude comes home from school with a

	PLUS	MINUS
FIRSTBORN	In control	Perfectionist
	Punctual	Moody
	Organized	Critical
	Conscientious	Stubborn
	Serious	Skeptical
	Scholastically minded	Tense
	Reliable	Driven
	Planner	Flawfinder
MIDDLE BORN	Intensely loyal	Feels inferior to others
	Good negotiator	Avoids confrontation
	Competitive	Feels squeezed and closed in
	Well adjusted	
	Social	Hides feelings
	Master of compromise	Easily embarrassed
	Peacemaker	
LAST BORN	Tolerant	Impulsive
	Personable	Irresponsible
	Sees others' point of view	Disorganized
	Easygoing	Manipulative
	Spontaneous	Self-centered
	Caring	Rebellious
	Affectionate	

picture of a horse she drew. She shows it to her mother, who oohs and ahhs and tells her daughter what a good artist she is. But when she shows the same picture to her big brother, he says, "It looks more like a frog to me. And it's not a very good frog, either!"

Well, one minute Gertrude is feeling very good about herself, and the next minute her ego has been crushed.

As a result of this kind of thing Last Borns are never really sure how to handle some of the situations life throws their way. They believe in themselves and have confidence in their abilities, but then they subconsciously remember the times when they were unable to do things as well as their older siblings. There is a residual feeling of inadequacy in almost all Last Borns, no matter how far they go in life.

Part of the reason, in fact, that the Last Born is likely to become the class clown is that he thinks this is the only way he can really compete and get the attention he needs.

If you are a Last Born, you are in company with Goldie Hawn, Charlie Chaplin, Billy Crystal, Jackie Gleason, Eddie Murphy, Teddy Kennedy, and, as I mentioned earlier, yours truly.

Notice the comedians, and then notice that it's "Eddie" rather than "Ed" Murphy, and "Billy" rather than "Bill" Crystal. I'm not saying that all comedians are Last Borns—just most of them. I can hear you saying that there must be some First Borns who are comedians. Sure 'nuff. Bill Cosby is a First Born, but please notice that he is not known as "Billy" Cosby, and if you watch the credits on his TV show, you'll see him listed as "William" with a doctorate degree following his name.

Cosby shows his Firstborn tendencies in other ways as well. For instance, he gave every one of his children a name beginning with the letter *E* as a reminder always to strive for excellence.

Talk about a Firstborn thing to do!

Birth Order and Romance

Now that we've concluded our brief tour of the birth orders, we're going to take a look at the way those birth orders fit—or don't fit —together when it comes to romance and marriage.

Coming up next, we'll pay special attention to what happens when similar birth orders attract.

PART TWO

For Firstborns Only

2

When Firstborns Collide

Are you a Firstborn? Are you looking for love, trying to sort out a complicated love life, or are you in the process of figuring out why love has been so hard to find all these years?

Well, before you know the type of person to be looking for, dating, or marrying, you'd better know yourself.

Self-delusions can be extremely dangerous when it comes to romance. Ask yourself these questions:

1. You're at a party. A handsome stranger approaches you and tells you your blouse is inside out. Do you:
    A. Laugh and tell him this is the new fashion, and by the way, could he bring you a soda?
    B. Bristle, throw your drink in his face, and stalk away to fix your blouse?
    C. Your blouse never would have been inside out in the first place so this is a ridiculous question.
2. It's Valentine's Day. Are you likely to:
    A. Send flowers to your sweetie?
    B. Hand her a card if you happen to see her that day?

   C. You've always hated this sappy holiday and you'd pre-
       fer to work late, thank you.
3. Your mate has left a trail of shoes, dirty socks, and other
   clothes all across the floor, leading up to the easy chair in
   front of the TV where he's fallen asleep and is snoring loudly.
   Do you:
   A. Kiss his forehead and take the precariously angled beer
       from his hand?
   B. Blow a police whistle close to his ear to let him know
       it's dinnertime?
   C. Your husband knows to go directly to the kitchen to
       prepare a Cordon Bleu meal for the family when he
       comes home, and his socks are never dirty anyway.

Okay, let's see how you did. If you answered A to all three of
these questions, rest assured that they will someday be naming a
high school after you, and the prefix in front of your name will be
Saint.

If you're more of a B person, lighten up a little, will ya?

And if you're the C type, I wonder if you've ever thought about
trying to get a job with the Marines—they can always use a good
drill sergeant!

I'm just having some fun, here, of course—but the truth is that
it's a grand idea to take a self-inventory before heading out on the
trail of romance.

Take a look at how you react in various situations and ask
yourself why. Make an inventory of your pet peeves—the things
about life that really bug you—and another list of the things you
really enjoy.

Once you really know who *you* are, then you can start worrying
about who your perfect partner might be.

Now, if you are a Firstborn, there are some general guidelines
regarding the best and worst possible mate for you.

Who should a Firstborn marry?

The absolutely best choice is a Last Born.

Who should a Firstborn stay away from?

The answer is—another Firstborn.

But the fact is that Firstborns often do wind up married to each other. And as they're standing at the altar during their wedding, they have no idea of the problems they're going to have to overcome to make their marriage work.

Have you ever taken a birth-order inventory of your friends? Not your acquaintances, now, but your close, personal friends.

If you do, you're likely to find that most of them are from your birth order. It really does seem to be true that birds of a feather will flock together.

That's because we tend to feel closer to those who share our interests—those who can understand what makes us tick.

In the same way, most people look for a lifetime partner who's pretty much the same as they are. But is that always a good idea?

The answer is no.

There are many dangers when two Firstborns wind up with each other. There are other, different dangers that result from the combination of two Middle Children or two Last Borns. Please remember that I'm not saying that two members of the same birth order should never become romantically involved—but there are special complications, and sooner or later such a relationship will come face-to-face with them.

Not long ago, after I spoke at a conference in California, I was confronted by a young man who was quite angry over what I had said about a marriage between two Firstborns being less than ideal.

"I think you're wrong in what you say about Firstborns," he challenged me. "My parents are both Firstborns, and they've been married for twenty-five years."

"Well, that's wonderful," I told him.

"Yes, and they get along great. I've never seen two people who were more in love."

My hat is off to these people, who have obviously loved each other enough to work at keeping their love and their marriage alive for twenty-five years. In this day that's quite an accomplishment for any couple. (We live in an era in which your refrigerator or oven range has a life span that is approximately double that of the average marriage.) For a couple consisting of two Firstborns, it's really remarkable. It shows that everything I am going to say in this book is subject to exceptions, but those exceptions do not come easily.

Before going any farther, let me explain that in this book I am writing for two quite different groups of people. The first group consists of single people who want to know who they ought to be dating—or at least who they ought to be considering as marriage material. The second group is made up of people who are already married but feel that a better understanding of how birth order affects romantic relationships will help to improve their marriage. So, if you're a Firstborn who happens to be dating another Firstborn, contemplating marriage to another Firstborn, or perhaps even married to another Firstborn, the next few pages are especially for you!

The Fighting Firsts: A Marriage or a War?

If I were to pick a romantic relationship that I would give the absolutely worst chance of succeeding, it would be one between two Firstborns, and especially between two Only Children or Super Firstborns.

If you want to pick the Firstborns out of a group of people, give them all something that has to be assembled, and see how they approach the task. The Firstborns won't do anything until they've had a chance to read the directions. The Middle Borns may take a cursory look at the directions, but they won't spend nearly the time with them that the Firstborns will. As for the Last Borns, they won't even notice that directions came with the thing, but will plunge right in and start attaching wing nut A to toggle bolt C.

You see, that's how Firstborns operate. You might consider

them people of the book. I'm sure Judge Wapner is a Firstborn. They want to make sure things are done right, and that includes everything from putting together a child's toy to keeping a marriage together.

What this means, of course, is that Firstborns are quicker to recognize problems and seek to overcome them.

If that's true, then why would I say that a relationship between two Firstborns is so difficult? Primarily because Firstborns in general are such hard-charging, stubborn, aggressive people. They know exactly how things ought to be.

The world of physics has long speculated over what the result would be when an irresistible force came into contact with an immovable object. If you want to know the answer to that question, all you have to do is take a look at two perfectionistic Firstborns who are dating or married to each other! I would say that the result is bound to be a lot of heat, light, and noise. In other words—an explosion!

Remember that there are two specific types of Firstborns. One is the hard-driven type who is desperately trying to climb to the top, whereas the other is the compliant type who only wants to please others.

This means there are two types of relationships that consist entirely of Firstborns or Only Children.

The first is the incident I just described, where immovable object and irresistible force come face-to-face. The second is where Mr. Aggressive is dating Miss Compliant (or vice versa), and the entire relationship becomes a bully-and-victim affair, where one partner seems to thrive on pushing the other one around, and the other one lets it happen. That's no basis for a relationship, and sooner or later it's going to fall apart. (If you'd like to do some additional reading on the subject, take a look at my book *The Pleasers: Women Who Can't Say No and the Men Who Control Them,* published by Dell.)

I've seen more than my share of both of these types of relationships.

Mr. Aggressive v.
Ms. Aggressive

I remember one Firstborn couple who, to all outward appearances, had it all.

The husband—I'll call him Harry—was an engineer for a huge mining firm. He made excellent money, had a large staff working under his direction, and seemed headed for a vice-president's position.

His wife, Elizabeth, had started her own interior decorating business and was doing quite well with that. They lived in a big house in one of the better neighborhoods in the city, they both drove fancy cars, and sent their two children to one of the best private schools in town.

They really did have it all—but the all they had was going quickly down the tubes. Both of them were so absorbed in their careers, and in their determination to reach the top, that they had very little time for each other, or for the children. And whose fault was that?

"He doesn't understand that my career is important to me," Elizabeth would say. "He's never there to give me the support and encouragement I need. All he thinks about is himself!"

"I'm never there to give her support?" Harry would respond. "I work twelve hours a day and then I come home to find the kids have no idea where their mother is, and ask me if I can fix them something for supper. What kind of support and encouragement is that?"

Now someone's bound to say, "Well, isn't this a common problem for two-career couples?" To some degree, yes, but not to the extent it would be a problem for two ladder-climbing, career-oriented Firstborns.

The truth is that for Harry and Elizabeth, the problem over their careers was only a symptom of a larger, deeper personality conflict—and it had everything to do with being hard-driving

Firstborns who never entered anything without striving to be the best at it.

They were both used to being the best, and neither one of them had quite come to the realization that marriage is a partnership—and not a competition where you have to finish ahead of your mate. Because of this they had been butting heads almost since the very first day of their marriage.

Were they being selfish? You bet they were. But both of them were being quite logical as well. Harry worked hard every day, and he felt that he had a right to expect things to be better taken care of at home. Simultaneously, however, Elizabeth's business was taking up an increasing amount of her own day, and it wasn't as if she was spending all that time at the beauty parlor or playing tennis at the country club.

Harry was making very good money, and so he saw no reason for Elizabeth to want to work in the first place. Elizabeth felt that she had been blessed with a designer's eye and skill, and saw no reason why she shouldn't find fulfillment in using those skills.

All of these things were true, but they didn't present any insurmountable problems. All that was called for to rectify the situation was a spirit of compromise. Fortunately, beneath all of their competing with each other and their complaining, Harry and Elizabeth really did love each other very much, and so were willing to work at it.

Harry realized he could do more around the house without complaining. For her part Elizabeth said she could cut back on the number of clients she was handling. She didn't really need to be as busy as she had been.

In the meantime both of them had to understand that it wasn't going to be very easy to change. They had both been aggressive and competitive since kindergarten, and probably before. The important thing, though, was that they were willing to attempt a compromise, and they both agreed to make allowances for the Firstborn nature of the other.

What can you do if you're an aggressive Firstborn who finds himself in a romantic relationship with someone just like you?

—You can make your relationship a number-one priority. Ask yourself how much energy you're investing into other areas of your life: your career? school? involvement in social or civic activities? Approach your relationship with the same sort of commitment, and you've taken a big step toward success.

—Take the first step toward compromise. I haven't seen a successful relationship yet that didn't involve a lot of give-and-take from both parties. It isn't easy for the aggressive Firstborn to compromise, but it can be done. Remember that things shouldn't always go your way—your partner has friends, obligations, and desires that are just as important as yours. Fight your feelings every once in a while and be the compromiser. At the same time try to convince your partner that he, too, needs to bend in order to make the relationship work.

—Talk to each other. Take time out from your busy schedules to sit and talk over a cup of coffee for at least thirty minutes each day. It doesn't matter when—whether it's easier to do it over breakfast or after dinner in the evening—as long as you do it. This is simple advice, I know, but you'd be surprised how hard it is for a couple of aggressive types to do something like this. It may mean letting something "important" go undone once in a while, but so what? There's nothing more important than love. And when you talk, do your best to be noncompetitive and unaggressive. Show some interest in your partner and some pleasure in her achievements.

Now, there are other problems that can arise when two perfectionist Firstborns marry.

For instance, I mentioned before that Firstborns tend to be organized and in control.

In the Bedroom with
Mr. and Mrs. Perfectionist

Another couple I counseled—Ronald and Barbara—were having major problems with regard to their sex life, and it was all because they were both meticulous Firstborns. Barbara, in fact, was an Only Child and, characteristically for that species, was superorganized. She had heard the saying "A place for everything and everything in its place," and when it came to making love to her husband, even that was to be done at a specific time, a specific place, and under specific conditions.

Barbara never wanted to make love on a weeknight, and mornings were out altogether. Friday and Saturday nights were fine, though, because they were part of the weekend—and in fact she expected her husband to be available every Friday and Saturday night.

Furthermore, Barbara insisted on being undressed and in bed ahead of her husband.

Now, from all this you might wonder if Barbara had some hangups about sex, or more specifically about her own body, but Ronald insisted that this wasn't the case. When the time for making love rolled around, they both had a great time. The two nights per week she allotted to this sort of romantic activity were certainly worth waiting for, as far as Ronald was concerned.

The big problem for him was that he wanted spontaneity.

"You know, Doc—like maybe snuggling up next to her on a Wednesday night and letting one thing lead to another."

Another problem stemmed directly from his Firstborn nature. He was beginning to see his wife's formulistic approach to sex as a rejection of him. He had worked hard all his life to be the best at everything he did, but he was one of those "discouraged" perfectionists. He had never quite measured up to the expectations of his authoritative and critical father. He had never quit trying to measure up, but his subconscious had begun telling him years ago that he was never going to make it.

As far as he was concerned, he must not be doing a very good job of keeping Barbara satisfied sexually. If he were better in bed, surely she would want to make love more often.

Ronald was wrong in his assessment. Barbara, in fact, thought their sex life was just fine. She said she enjoyed making love—but she wanted to do it on her terms.

Ronald, because he felt rejected by Barbara, began to find fault and pick at her. He criticized her housework and her cooking. Interestingly enough, the house was almost too neat to suit him, and he complained that it was like living in a sterilized clinic. Barbara, you see, was as meticulous about keeping the house neat and clean and planning her weekly menu as she was about what went on in the bedroom. She even wiped the telephone clean after every use. Talk about a Firstborn.

Now, I realize that the story of Barbara and Ronald might sound extreme. Most "controllers" don't go to the lengths Barbara did, and it's unusual to find someone of Ronald's temperament married to someone like her. But the Firstborn controller is going to see a reflection of himself in Barbara's behavior, while the Firstborn discouraged perfectionist will certainly see himself in Ronald's reaction to that behavior.

What could Ronald and Barbara—or any other similar couple —do to improve their marriage?

Several things:

1. Admit out loud to each other that they were both perfectionists and that this was causing trouble between them.
2. Agree that they would be willing to attempt to change their attitudes and habits, while acknowledging that it wouldn't always happen without effort.
3. Try to understand that each of them has an ingrained approach to life that was not meant to be hurtful or vindictive.
4. Try to talk things out openly, rather than allowing resentments to build up.

The hardest thing for Barbara to do was to change her behavior. She agreed with me that she would take a first step by leaving the house in the morning to visit a friend *before* she had made the beds. It wasn't easy at all, but she gritted her teeth and did it. That may sound like one small step to you, but it was one giant leap for Barbara-kind.

For his part Ronald agreed that he would attempt to stop reading between the lines and seeing everything as a criticism of him as a person. Even when he did feel hurt, he was to stop and think before he lashed out.

Ronald and Barbara were able to chip away at their problems and, for the most part, overcome them. They weren't going to change overnight into a laid-back pair who just took life as it came. But they could, and did, concentrate on straightening up the areas that were placing the most pressure on their marriage.

In fact Barbara laughingly admitted, blushing as she did, that she and her husband had actually made love on a Tuesday evening. It had seemed a little strange at first, she told me, but after a while she forgot all about the fact that it was a weeknight, and really enjoyed herself!

Ronald must have been proud.

In the years I've been involved in private psychological practice, I have counseled hundreds of people with sexual problems in their marriages. The majority of them came from marriages involving at least one Firstborn, and the cause of the problem was almost always similar to what was going on in Barbara and Ronald's marriage. There was too much organization regarding the bedroom, fear of rejection, or anger over perceived rejection.

Do Barbara and Ronald's problems sound a bit extreme to you?

If so, ask yourself the following questions:

—Do you find it hard to put down that grocery list you've been working on when your husband starts nibbling on the back of your neck?

—When your wife is modeling a sexy new nightie, do you look up from your paperwork and mumble, "Very nice, dear"?

—Does your sex life lack spontaneity and variety?

—How long has it been since you've made love in the middle of the day, or with the light on?

If any of these situations seems familiar, you need to work at changing yourself and/or your partner.

Insofar as changing your behavior is concerned, that involves simply making up your mind to do it.

As in "When my husband is being affectionate I will stop planning my menu for the following week."

And "When my wife is showing me her sexy new gown, I'll take more than a passing interest."

If you want your partner to change, the best thing you can do is learn to communicate. I know it's not always easy for couples to talk about sex, but if you can't say it out loud, surely you can write a note. And remember, when you're talking about sex, you've got to make your partner feel desired.

Do you love him? Then tell him so. Do you like for him to hold you in his arms? Tell him that too. Let him know that you love being with him and making love to him—and once you've let him know that this is true, you can tell him what's missing in your love life, or what would really make you happy in this part of your life together.

You can also change your love life by such "sexy" activities as renting a hotel room in the middle of the week and sneaking off for a naughty rendezvous. If you're the one who's overly organized, it may really go against your feelings to do something like this. But sometimes the best thing you can do is to go against those feelings. If your partner is the one who seems to be rigid and inflexible, your "surprise" is likely to catch him with his defenses down. And you very well might precipitate a drastic change in his behavior and outlook.

One woman surprised her overly organized and predictable husband with a note delivered with dessert which said, *Meet me upstairs at nine-thirty.* What he found at nine-thirty was his wife in a sexy new gown, a bottle of champagne resting in a bucket of ice, two glasses on the table by the bed, and the soft, flickering light from a dozen candles placed throughout the room.

A most pleasant discovery it was—and Mr. and Mrs. Predictable reportedly had a very wild and enjoyable time.

The Pleaser and
the Controller

A relationship between two Firstborns who have developed pretty much along the same lines is hard enough to deal with. But when you have one partner who is a compliant pleaser type, and the other is the dominant, take-charge person who never gives a moment's thought to the other person's desires and needs, you've really got yourself a disaster.

Usually, in a relationship of this sort, the compliant one will be the wife, who is dominated by her controller, aggressive husband. Notice that I said "usually" and not "always," because there are cases where a mild-mannered man who wants everyone to be happy is doing his best to please a domineering woman. But of the many cases of pleaser-controller relationships that I've seen over the years, I'd say that fewer than one in twenty fits this description.

Many pleaser-controller relationships come to mind, but I especially remember Janet, who was an intelligent, articulate, and attractive young woman—a Firstborn—teamed up with a demanding, domineering man who expected her to wait on him constantly. He was a man who rarely thanked her or complimented her when she did something well, but who was always quick to criticize her when he believed she had failed in some manner, and he didn't mind criticizing her in front of others.

He saw no reason to change things, of course. Why should he? Everything was going exactly the way he wanted it to go. Only, he didn't have someone who was his equal partner. He had a woman who was at his beck and call, and he could have gotten that by hiring a maid.

In looking back over Janet's life it quickly became apparent to me that she had the same sort of relationship with her husband that she had always had with her father.

"I tried so hard to please him," she said of her father, "but I guess I never did a very good job of it."

Her father had been the type who, when Janet brought home a report card with five A's, a B, and a C, wouldn't say a word about the good grades. He would focus immediately on the C and tell her that she wouldn't get such a bad grade if she paid more attention in class, or if she weren't so lazy.

It wasn't only when she was young and in school that she wanted to please her father and couldn't, but her quest to make him proud of her continued well into her adult years. She was excited when an article she had written was published in a regional magazine. She sent it to her parents, and you can guess what happened. Mom read it and loved it, but Dad somehow never had the time to read his daughter's work. She landed a big part in a community theater production and invited her parents to come on opening night. They promised her they'd be there, but at the last minute "something came up" and they stayed away.

Now you're probably thinking that her father sounds like a cruel and heartless man. I've known enough men just like him, though, to believe that he really did love his daughter, and he wanted her to have the best in life. But for some reason those loving, warm feelings were bottled up inside of him and he could never bring himself to let them be seen.

Now, one would think that Janet would eventually realize that the problem was with her father rather than with herself. And one would also think that when Janet picked a man to marry, she would try to find someone who was everything her father was not.

Unfortunately it didn't work that way in Janet's life.

Janet's choice of a mate was fairly typical of a compliant First-born. Invariably women such as Janet will choose to marry men who are carbon copies of their fathers. Perhaps it is a continuation of the lifelong quest to gain approval from Daddy.

Whatever the reason, thousands of compliant Firstborn women have escaped from unpleasant relationships with their fathers, only to find themselves in unpleasant relationships with their mates.

Janet's problem wasn't completely with her man, but with herself as well. Nobody can push you around unless you allow it to happen. If you make a habit of lying down on the floor and trying to disguise yourself as a doormat, people are going to walk all over you. If you learn to stand up for yourself, people will be less inclined to take advantage of you.

Janet had to learn that she was her partner's equal in every respect. She had to stop waiting on him and let him know, as forcefully as she could, that she expected him to do things for himself.

There was no guarantee that he would change. After all, Janet could not be responsible for the way he acted. But she could be responsible for herself. Changing her own actions was the best thing she, or any compliant Firstborn who is involved with a controller type, could do.

Janet's husband had a habit of not letting her know what time he was coming home from work. One night it might be five-thirty and the next night it would be seven. As far as he was concerned, no matter what time he came home dinner should be ready for him as soon as he walked through the door.

I instructed Janet to tell him that dinner would be served at six o'clock every night. If he phoned her and let her know he was going to be late, she would do her best to wait for him. If, on the other hand, he came home early, he would just have to wait until six o'clock.

Her words didn't change the man's behavior. Just a few nights later he came home after seven without calling to tell her he'd be late. She went ahead and fed the kids at six, as she had said she would, and then cleaned the table and put away the dishes.

When hubby came home growling and fuming and demanding his supper, she told him she was sorry, but he'd have to find his own dinner tonight. She reminded him that dinner was going to be served at six o'clock, and unless he had a very good excuse for coming home late, that's just the way it was going to be. Again, she wasn't nasty about it, but she was firm. If he wanted dinner, he knew where the kitchen was, and there was no reason he couldn't fix it for himself.

Hubby wound up having a peanut-butter-and-jelly sandwich for dinner and went to bed angry. Now, as I said earlier, there was no guarantee that her husband would change. In fact, it's possible that he could become even more abusive and angry than he already was. But Janet had reached the point where she knew something had to happen. She was not going to continue to live with the man the way he was. Either things were going to change or she was going to get out of the marriage.

I wouldn't give a hundred percent guarantee, but I would suspect that eighty-five to ninety percent of the time, a change in the attitude of the pleaser is going to cause a change in the attitude of the controller. That's exactly what happened in Janet's case.

Her husband, despite all his fuming and anger, suddenly began to treat her with respect. She couldn't believe it when, a week or so after the peanut-butter-and-jelly episode, he called her and told her he wasn't going to be home until six-thirty. He even explained why, telling her he had some paperwork the boss wanted him to finish. Never before had he seemed to think she deserved the least bit of explanation. Why he was late was his business and his business alone.

Part of the problem for her Firstborn hubby, you see, was that he had been brought up to have a very high opinion of himself. He had been praised and encouraged and taught that he was somebody special, and the result had been that he had not been very thoughtful or patient with others.

How to Spot a Controller

A compliant Firstborn woman very often winds up with a man who is a textbook controller. Unfortunately she usually won't know what she's getting herself into until it's too late. Here is a little quiz to let you know if the man you're interested in is a controller (and, of course, the sexual roles may be reversed). Answer the following questions with "always," "sometimes," "seldom," and "never," with respective scores of 4, 3, 2, and 1 points:

1. When he's behind the wheel of the car, does he often yell at the other drivers on the road?
2. When you and he are going somewhere by car, does he insist on driving?
3. When he's traveling by car with a group of other people, is he the one who winds up doing the driving?
4. Does he speak with disrespect or anger about other women who have been part of his life? (Including his mother, sister, co-worker, et cetera.)
5. If you do something he doesn't like, does he become angry to the point of yelling or becoming physically violent?
6. Does he make sexual demands upon you?
7. Does his sense of humor rely on getting laughs at your expense, or at the expense of others?
8. If he makes a mistake, does he find a way to blame it on others who "don't know what they're doing"?
9. Does he always have to win in competitive activities?
10. Does he usually "get his way" deciding when and where you will eat, where you will go, and what you will do?

Scoring:

34–40 Points: A Super Controller who will be hard to deal with on any basis, long or short term.

28–33 Points: A "typical" controller who quite possibly can be confronted and asked to change.

20–27 Points: Shows a balance between control and flexibility, probably a good bet for a husband.

19 and Under: Probably not a controller, but take another look at the questions he scored highest on, just to make sure.

Now remember that a controller isn't always obvious in his behavior. But there are always clues:

—Does he insist that you spend most of your time with his friends while yours are feeling neglected?

—Do you always have to wait for him to call you because he doesn't like it when you call him?

—Do you always celebrate holidays the way his family did, never mind your family's traditions?

—Does he insist upon disciplining the kids his way because you're too lenient?

If this sounds like your partner, then you could be involved with a controller.

Are You a Pleaser?

Now that we've taken a look at how to spot the controller, it's time for a self-inventory to see if you might have the opposite problem. Do people treat you as if you had WELCOME stamped across your forehead in big block letters? If they do, maybe it's because you do a pretty good impression of a doormat.

Answer these questions the same as the previous quiz, "always," "sometimes," "seldom," and "never."

1. If you're in a group going out for dinner, how often do you get to choose the restaurant?
2. If you order chicken and the waiter brings you a seafood platter, will you tell him that he hasn't brought you what you ordered?
3. If you're with people who begin talking about politics, and you don't agree with what's being said, will you speak up and give your opinion?
4. If it's past midnight, and your next-door neighbor is playing his stereo much too loud, will you call and ask him to tone it down?
5. If you're in the middle of an important project, and a friend calls "just to chat," will you tell him that you don't have time to talk right now?
6. If the boss asks for volunteers to work late and get that special project wrapped up, do you find your hand going up to volunteer before you've really even had time to think about it?

7. If you're traveling by car and someone cuts you off and then gestures angrily at you, do you automatically assume that you did something wrong?

8. If someone does something that makes you angry, do you always feel bad about it later on and worry that you made a fool of yourself?

9. Do you find yourself taking the blame for things that weren't your fault and apologizing for things you didn't do?

10. Do you daydream about being someone "important"?

You can score this in the same way as the "controller" quiz, but if you saw yourself one too many times in this one, it's time to resolve that you're going to change!

Before we move on, let's take a look at some other typical problems that arise in a relationship between two Firstborns:

Mr. and Mrs. Overcommitted

A man and a woman can't build a lasting, loving relationship with each other if they're too busy with other things to spend any time with each other—and that's a frequent problem when two achievement-oriented Firstborns team up.

Oscar and Rhonda's marriage was in trouble, and no wonder— they hardly ever saw each other, unless it was at a PTA meeting or another such gathering. They were two extremely conscientious people, who knew the importance of being active in their local community. But their involvement in a variety of important programs was coming at the expense of their marital happiness. What was a couple like this one to do?

1. Admit that something had to change. They could start by admitting to themselves and each other that nothing else was as important as saving their marriage.

2. Cut back on their obligations. They should both make a conscious effort to cut back on the number of outside activities in

which they were involved. They could sit down together, make a list of these outside "obligations," and then decide where they could cut back. I went so far as to suggest that Rhonda take a look at Oscar's list, and vice versa. If you're too close to know where to cut back, let your mate help you decide. Let me say, too, that there would have to be an honest commitment on the part of both partners to cut back. I don't believe in meeting someone halfway either. Instead, try to give seventy or eighty percent, and expect your partner to come the rest of the way. If you think you're giving seventy percent, chances are good that what you're really doing is giving enough to meet someone halfway.

3. Spend time together. Rhonda and Oscar also needed to learn the importance of taking some time for themselves. This is important in every marriage, but especially in the case of two hard-driving Firstborns. Rhonda and Oscar both saw life as one "duty" piled on top of another, but one "duty" they had been overlooking was spending time with each other. Oscar was the type of man who was never very far from his "daily reminder," which was loaded with umpteen dozen things he needed to do. I suggested that he write his wife's name down on his daily schedule, just to remember that he needed to make time for her. Actually, because Firstborns tend to be such driven and list-oriented people, it is a pretty good idea for such a husband and wife to actually schedule time to spend together.

4. Let someone else do it. Does that sound selfish? Does it sound as if I'm promoting apathy? Well, the truth is that the Firstborn sometimes has to be prodded to let the world take a few spins without him. Rhonda and Oscar both had to promise me that they weren't going to volunteer for any other committees or extra assignments until they had cut back on their present commitments.

5. Make sure your children are not overinvolved. If they're involved in too many activities someone—and most probably

Mom—is going to go bonkers shuttling the ankle-biter battalion back and forth in her yellow minivan. I believe limiting your children to two outside activities per semester is good for them and good for Mom and Dad as well!

Mr. "Doesn't Appreciate Anything" and Mrs. Achiever

Remember the song "Little Things Mean a Lot?" Well, it's true. The little things can be integral in building a lasting marriage, and they can help to tear it down.

I counsel hundreds of couples whose marriages are crumbling, not because of any great problems, but because the little things have piled up over the years, and now there's a mountain of resentment blocking the path to lasting happiness.

In the San Francisco area we saw what happens when tensions are allowed to build, build, and build some more over a period of time. The San Andreas Fault stretched and strained and groaned —and then when the tension became too great, the great fault slipped, resulting in a massive earthquake. Buildings collapsed, bridges fell down, and dozens of people were killed. Marriages are every bit as fragile as the buildings and highways that collapsed in San Francisco, and unless both partners work at eliminating tension, a collapse is going to come.

One problem that creates tremendous tension in Firstborn marriages is when one partner is perfectionistic and expects too much from the other. Firstborns have a tendency to place unreasonable demands upon their own shoulders, but they can be just as demanding of others.

Listen to these words, from Linda, and see if they don't hit home: "He doesn't seem to appreciate anything I do. I don't mind doing things for him—but it would sure be nice to know that he appreciated me."

Linda was an intelligent, hardworking Firstborn who expected a great deal from herself, but her husband always seemed to expect more. She needed appreciation and understanding and she wasn't getting either from him, because he expected nothing but perfection from himself or his wife. What she really needed was to have someone who would get her to relax once in a while and take life a little bit easier—but what she had instead was someone who was always urging her to new heights, whether in her job, her educational goals, her cooking, or any other area of her life.

What could someone like Linda do?

1. Tell her husband how she felt. Simple and direct communication is the most important step for any man or woman who is seeing his marriage give way under an avalanche of "little things." But I also realize that it's easier to tell someone to communicate with her mate than it may be for her to do it.

   I am still amazed, after all my years in private practice, that some married couples find it so hard to communicate. How can you sleep with someone night after night, see them staring across the breakfast table at you every morning with messed-up hair and bleary eyes, even share a bathroom with each other, and still not be able to talk to each other? Yet my experience tells me that this is true all too often. If you can't talk to someone, though, you can certainly write them a note.

   I have suggested that couples buy a clear bowl—a fishbowl works very well—and place it in a location where each will see it every day. Then they can buy different-colored pads of paper—perhaps pink for her and blue for him. When she wants to tell him something, she writes it on a pink piece of paper and puts it in the bowl, and vice versa for him. It may sound crazy, but the idea has helped many couples, including Linda and her husband.

2. Learn to be forgiving. Linda's husband wasn't going to change overnight, no matter how much she wanted him to. What she needed was to work at changing him, but realize that it was going to take time, and try her best to forgive him when he let her down.

3. Lower your own sights. Most of the pressure Linda was feeling came from within herself instead of her husband. He was going to be the same old Tom whether or not she got the next big promotion, so why was she continuing to beat her head against that old wall? True, he was always there to urge her on to newer and greater heights, but her attitude and behavior had always egged him on. She had to take it easier on herself.

I admit that it's not always easy to lower your sights. It takes self-discipline. But if you have to grit your teeth to force yourself to stop and smell the roses, then grit away!

As we've talked about a relationship between two Firstborns, we've seen that a marriage between two such people is not likely to be a lifelong day at the beach.

But it doesn't have to be a painful experience either.

They say it takes a heap o' lovin' to make a house a home, and it will take an even bigger heap o' lovin' to turn a romantic entanglement between two Firstborns into paradise, but it can be done, no doubt about it. Yes, I do know happily married couples who are both Firstborns, and some of them have been married since before Elvis Presley was a star—and that's a long, long time!

With love, a willingness to change, a willingness to be changed, a healthy sense of humor, and a desire to work hard, two Firstborns can do just fine.

Coming up next, we'll take a look at the very best choices a Firstborn can make when it comes to romance and marriage.

3

The Firstborn Takes a Wife (or a Husband)

Are you paying close attention, Mr. or Ms. Firstborn? I hope so, because I'm about to tell you how to find the girl or guy of your dreams.

And even if you're not a Firstborn, I hope you're paying attention, too, because you're going to gain some insights into the often troubling world of romantic relationships—especially if you're tangled up with a Firstborn, or want to be.

My goal is to turn you into a first-rate romantic detective, so that you'll be able to look at any romantic relationship and be able to tell—with a very high rate of accuracy—whether it's going to work and why or why not.

Before I begin, though, I'm sure there are some skeptics out there who are saying, "What you're going to tell us may look terrific in theory, but does it work in the real world?"

Well, to any such doubting Thomases, I am happy to say that as an amateur matchmaker, I am batting a cool 1.000. That's right. As a psychologist I spend a great deal of my time seeking to help married couples stay married; but I can think of only one instance in which I made an attempt at getting two people together, and I had overwhelming success.

There was a single gentleman—a widower—with two young daughters, who was attending the same church I was attending. This man was absolutely terrific with his daughters. He was gentle, affectionate, and I knew he was good husband material because of that.

At the same time there was a young woman in the church who seemed to be a good match for him. I talked to them individually, not about each other, but primarily about the subject of birth orders. He was a Firstborn who had younger sisters, while she was the only girl and Last Born among four children. Aha! It looked like a perfect fit to me!

Because the congregation was a large one, they had never had the opportunity to meet each other. I figured it was about time that opportunity presented itself.

All I did, really, was to introduce them and then stand back and wait for the inevitable. I didn't have to wait long.

I could see after the first two or three dates that they were headed in the direction of the altar.

Today that couple is very happily married. So . . . yes, I've spent several years of my life researching the subject of birth order, and I know its importance within romantic relationships. Yes, I have a doctorate in psychology, and I know all the studies that have been undertaken on various aspects of birth order, and I can quote formulas and variables to you until your head starts spinning or you fall asleep—whichever comes first.

But on the other hand, I've also spent a little bit of time playing the role of matchmaker—and I'll have to tell you that I have a much better record than *The Dating Game!*

Your Perfect Match

If you're a Firstborn who's looking for a long-lasting honeymoon, I recommend—first of all—that you consider a marriage of mixed birth orders.

The very best choice for you, if you're a Firstborn, is to marry a Last Born. Not only is this the best combination for you, but it is actually the very best marriage combination of all when it comes to birth order.

Actually, though, because there are so many different types of Firstborns and Last Borns, it's really not a simple matter of saying that Firstborn–Last Born marriages are best, because there are varieties of these marriages that are better than others.

Before we get down to specifics, I want to remind you again that birth order is not the be-all and end-all of making a great match. My own Firstborn sister Sally is a case in point. Sally's husband, Wes, is also a Firstborn, and the two of them have built a happy, loving marriage and have raised three great kids as well. They've worked hard at their marriage, and their relationship has undoubtedly been strengthened by the fact that they share a common faith.

Birth order is not a final determining factor as to whether or not a marriage is going to work. But it is an excellent indicator of problems that you might discover in your relationships with others as you go through life. An understanding of birth order will show you what problems you are likely to have, or even create for yourself, and it will also help you to understand what problems others might face.

I would never tell a couple of Firstborns who were having problems that "you might as well go ahead and get a divorce, because your birth orders just aren't compatible." It takes a tremendous amount of hard work to make any marriage successful—even if your birth orders go together like lox and bagels.

But if you are a Firstborn who is looking for your very best partner, here are what a number of psychologists, myself included, believe to be the very best birth-order combinations:

1. The Firstborn female who has brothers with the Last-Born male who has sisters.
2. The Firstborn male who has brothers with the Last-Born female who has brothers.
3. The Firstborn male who has younger sisters with a Last-Born female with older brothers.
4. Any Firstborn female with any Last-Born male.

Psychologist Walter Toman is widely respected for his extensive research into the effects of birth order. In his book *Family Constellation* he explains how his study of more than three thousand families led him to decide that the birth-order combinations listed above make the best marriages.[1]

At the University of Wisconsin, Dr. Theodore D. Kemper conducted a study of 256 business executives and their wives.[2] His study also revealed certain birth-order combinations that seem to make the best marriages. The four birth-order combinations listed above come out of the research done by Drs. Toman and Kemper, as well as my own research and experience based on nearly twenty years as a practicing psychologist.

I would add to what my two distinguished colleagues have said, though, the observation that any Firstborn–Last-Born combination is likely to work very well.

Let's take a closer look at these combinations and see why they work so well. Taking a look, first of all, at the general Firstborn–Last-Born combination.

Any Firstborn–Last-Born Combination

This combination works very well as long as the partners are able to accept each other's differences and learn from each other.

Remember that as the oldest child, you're likely to be serious and scholarly—the type who has to have a corporate ladder to climb and who will be a nervous wreck if there isn't one to climb.

The youngest, though, is likely to be a fun-loving sort who doesn't think life is to be taken too seriously.

Obviously both of these views of life are going to create problems if they're allowed to go unchallenged. Unless your view of life

BEST RELATIONSHIP
COMBINATIONS FOR FIRSTBORNS

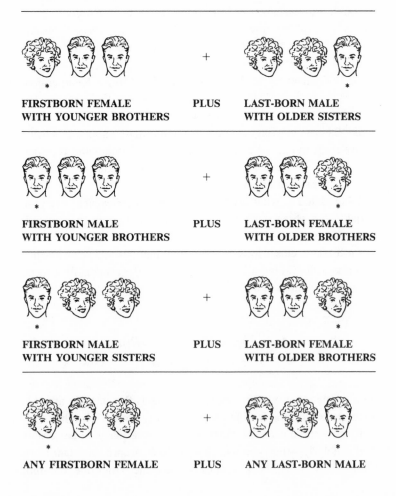

FIRSTBORN FEMALE WITH YOUNGER BROTHERS	PLUS	LAST-BORN MALE WITH OLDER SISTERS
FIRSTBORN MALE WITH YOUNGER BROTHERS	PLUS	LAST-BORN FEMALE WITH OLDER BROTHERS
FIRSTBORN MALE WITH YOUNGER SISTERS	PLUS	LAST-BORN FEMALE WITH OLDER BROTHERS
ANY FIRSTBORN FEMALE	PLUS	ANY LAST-BORN MALE

as the Firstborn is challenged, you're likely to work and worry yourself into an early grave—or at the very least a cold, joyless existence. You'll eventually become as warm and full of life as a robot. The Last Born will laugh himself silly, take life easy, and watch others pass him on the road to success. One of these years he'll wake up to wonder where his youth went and why none of his dreams ever came true.

The Firstborn, you see, needs someone to show him the pleasures of sunsets, rainbows, and remind him that it can be fun to let his mind wander and dream about all the wonderful things he'd like to do. The Last Born needs someone to show him that while having fun and daydreaming are wonderful things to do, it takes hard work and perseverance to turn those daydreams into reality.

You know, our society has traditionally taken a dim view of anyone who doesn't work hard to make a success of himself. Even the old fairy tales reflect this view.

Consider the story of the tortoise and the hare. The hare was a happy-go-lucky guy who could have run circles around that old turtle if he'd taken himself more seriously. The tortoise, on the other hand, didn't have much going for him when it came to speed, but he kept going, kept those old legs moving—one, two, three, four—one, two, three, four—and he eventually crossed the finish line well ahead of Mr. Speedy.

Consider also the three little pigs and the big, bad wolf. Two of the pigs were silly types who liked to sing and dance all day long. If they had worked hard to construct houses that were sturdy and safe, the wolf never would have been able to huff and puff and blow them down. It was only their hardworking, industrious brother, who took the time to build a house out of bricks, who was safe.

And then, of course, there is the story of the ant and the bumblebee. During the summer the bumblebee did nothing but buzz around all day smelling the flowers and feeling the sunshine on his back, while the ant worked hard all day long, carrying food down into his nest so he'd be ready when winter came. And when it did come, it came with a vengeance, catching poor old bumblebee completely unprepared.

Why am I talking about all of these old fairy tales and fables? Because it seems to me that our society has always encouraged Firstborns in their vices. No wonder we have so many workaholic Firstborns among us, working hard to earn their ulcers, wrinkled brows, and gray hairs! We encourage the hard workers while we look down upon those who seem to take a lighter approach to life.

The truth is, though, that life, to be complete, requires both hard work and the ability to stop and take it easy every once in a while. Every driven Firstborn should be thankful for what he can learn from a fun-loving Last Born.

If you're a Firstborn, you're likely to be:

—punctual

—moody

—organized

—critical of others

—stubborn

—competent

—perfectionistic

—someone who dislikes surprises

—someone who wants to see things done right the first time

You're likely, then, to need the balance offered by a partner who:

—doesn't think being late is a cardinal sin

—is easygoing

—doesn't mind an occasional mess

—is tolerant of others

—is capable of changing his mind and seeing the other fellow's point of view

—can be spontaneous and "spur of the moment" in his approach to life

—knows that everyone makes mistakes, including himself, and that they can always be corrected later

If you're a good romantic detective, and you spot someone who has those qualities, chances are he'll be a Last Born. You've seen someone who will be a good marriage partner for you. And, if you're not interested in marriage, you've at least come across someone who ought to be a fun date.

The reason a marriage made up of two Firstborns is likely to turn into a battleground is that both partners are so much alike. They are more likely to be involved in a heated, head-to-head competition than in a partnership based on sharing and considering the other person's needs first.

The reason that a marriage between two Last Borns runs into problems is that there is no one to say, "Don't you think we'd better start planning for the future?" If one of them has an urge to take a trip to the Bahamas and blow a month's pay, the other is likely to go along with it, and sooner or later they'll find themselves in financial trouble.

But put one of each together, and you've got a terrific balance. It's not a matter of all work and no play, but neither is it a matter of all play and no work.

Consider what happens to this planet of ours as it travels through space. The gravitational pull from the sun keeps the earth in its orbit. On the other hand the centrifugal force of the earth's motion through space counterbalances the sun's gravitational pull. If there were no centrifugal force, the sun's gravity would pull the earth on into the sun and we would all be turned into toasted marshmallows. On the other hand, if there were no gravity from the sun, the earth's centrifugal force would see us spinning on out into deep space, where we'd have icicles suspended from our ears in no time.

Balance is the key.

When it comes to Firstborn–Last-Born marriages, the partners have to respect each other enough to admit that the other has something of value to offer.

When I think of how a First and Last marriage can work, I consider John and Elizabeth, who married when both were in their middle thirties.

John was a Firstborn who developed the personality pattern that I refer to as "discouraged perfectionist." The discouraged perfectionist is different from the perfectionist in that he is never satisfied. Whatever he does, he always goes away thinking that he could have done it better. He is never able to settle for being number two in anything and doesn't think that merely being excellent is good enough.

John grew up trying to please a domineering father who always concentrated on the negative and never seemed to notice the good. No matter what it was—scholastic achievement, athletic performance, or any task he was trying to accomplish—John's dad always let him know he could have done it better.

Like most Firstborns John was expected to set a sterling example for his younger brothers and sisters. He had been expected to act like an adult from the time he was just a kid. He was actually a pretty talented guy, but he was filled with feelings of insecurity and inadequacy, and you could see it just by the way he stood— shoulders slouched, back slightly bent, head down. He was five eleven but looked to be about five eight or so, just because of the way he stood.

At least that's the way he was before he married Last-Born Elizabeth.

The first thing anyone noticed about Elizabeth was her laugh. She laughed all the time, but it wasn't an obtrusive, awkward laugh. It was an infectious laugh that made everyone who heard it want to laugh right along with her. I'm sure it was that laugh that attracted John to her in the first place.

Now, Last Borns make terrific salesmen, and this was the case with Elizabeth. She was the sort of person who could have charmed the Eskimos into buying ice in the wintertime. When she set her immense talents to work in an effort to sell John to himself, it was only a matter of time before he came to believe in himself almost as much as she did.

For one thing, John had always been a terrible procrastinator, which is a common characteristic of a discouraged perfectionist. Anything he wants to do, he wants to do perfectly. But because he's afraid he won't be perfect, he has an extremely hard time getting started on a task. In a work situation the discouraged perfectionist is apt to overextend himself by volunteering for just about every project that comes along. He does this to prove his worth, both to himself and to others, but then he'll let things go because when it comes down to actually doing the work, he's so afraid he'll fail that he can't even bring himself to start.

It was this particular trait of John's that Elizabeth went to work on. She helped him see that even if he did fail once or twice, it wouldn't be the biggest disaster in the world.

She got him to see things that no one else could have helped him to see. But because he loved and respected her so much, and because of her good-humored attitude about things, she enabled him to take a more realistic attitude about what others expected of him, and gently helped him to lower his expectations regarding his own performance. She teased him by telling him that it didn't really matter what anyone else thought of him anyway. She was the only one who mattered, and it wasn't possible for him to ever do anything to let her down.

She performed miracles in his life. He actually seemed to be growing taller, but it was only because he was feeling better about who and what he was. He was free, for the first time in his life, just to be himself.

Someone might ask, "Well, didn't Elizabeth get anything out of the marriage? It sounds to me as if she gave and gave and gave, while John just took everything she had to offer."

My answer is that Elizabeth probably did the lion's share of giving in the marriage, at least at first. But she did benefit from John's Firstborn tendencies.

For one thing, John had a tremendous intellect. He had the ability to go far in the corporate world but had always been held back by his own feelings of inadequacy. It is true, for instance, that other people will tend to believe about you what you believe about yourself. Because John had never believed in his own abilities, no one else had ever believed in them either, and he had been overlooked and seemed to be stagnating in his job. It was Elizabeth who helped to instill self-confidence in him, but once that happened, she, too, reaped the benefits of John's quick ascension of the corporate ladder.

And there were other benefits besides the financial ones. For instance, she also benefited from the fact that John was more at ease with himself because his self-confidence displayed itself in his approach to life. He laughed more easily and often, even developing the ability to laugh at himself when he was wrong. He also seemed to have more energy to get out and experience things, whereas before he had often been depressed and didn't feel like doing much of anything except sitting around the house.

John also helped her inject more organization into her life. She was the sort of person who tried to remember everything she had to do. She would often get to the end of the day and realize there were several things that had completely slipped her mind. John had always been a list keeper, as many Firstborns are, and he helped her to see how keeping a list of things to be done during the day could be helpful to her. She didn't overwhelm herself with a list—as John would have done—but by keeping a daily calendar in which she wrote down the most important of her appointments and tasks to be accomplished, she made much better use of her time.

All in all John and Elizabeth made a pretty terrific, and very happy, team.

Firstborn Female–
Last-Born Male

David is a Last Born who, like me, delighted in being the class clown when he was younger. He remembers especially that in the sixth grade he spent more time sitting out in the hall than he did in his own classroom. If there was a smart remark to be made or an elaborate stunt to pull on the teacher, he was likely to be the one to do it.

Diane was as much like that as a Porsche is like a Chevy pickup truck. She was a straight A student who was usually the apple of her teacher's eye. She still has a scrapbook full of certificates and awards she won. There are awards for science fairs, spelling bees, math competitions. You name it and she won it. Among those souvenirs and reminders of her triumphs there are several citizenship awards attesting to the fact that she was always a "good citizen."

Talk about the attraction of opposites!

Now, even though David has long since dispensed with the idea of being a clown all his life, he still demonstrates many of the qualities of the typical Last Born. For instance, he admits that he finds himself virtually unable to worry about things.

"I try real hard," he says. "I know there are things I should be worrying about, but I just don't seem to have the ability to worry about them."

Diane, on the other hand, is like many other Firstborns, in that she sees every problem coming a hundred miles away. She is the type who wants to plan carefully for every situation, and if Plan A doesn't work out, she's got Plans B through Z waiting in the wings.

When they first got married, they admit that their divergent personalities caused them a few problems.

Among Diane's Firstborn tendencies is a desire to do everything in the shortest, best, and most direct way possible. This attitude is quite common to Firstborns, who tend to be extremely well organized and predictable in their routines. This overwhelming desire to be efficient manifested itself in her knowledge of the roads and streets in the city where they lived. If she and her husband were going anywhere by car, even if just to the store to buy a loaf of bread, she knew the exact route to take, and any deviation from that route would cause her blood pressure to rise.

David, on the other hand, was so laid back that he usually didn't know which way he was going to go until he came to a fork in the road. If there were three different ways to get to the same store, he'd probably go one way and come home another. If he went the longest, most time-consuming way, it didn't matter to him, because he'd just enjoy the ride.

Diane would say, "Why are you going this way?"

"I don't know. Why do you ask?"

"This is a lot longer!"

"Really?"

"Yeah. A *lot* longer!"

"Well, I don't know, I just kind of wanted to go this way."

"I don't understand. Why? Why would you want to go this way when it's going to take an extra three minutes?"

She couldn't seem to understand that her husband didn't really have a plan, and it didn't matter much to him as long as he eventually reached his destination. At the same time, he couldn't understand what the big deal was about an extra mile or two and an extra few minutes. If there had been some emergency, he obviously would have taken the shortest route, but if there wasn't, why worry about it?

But it wasn't only the circuitous routes he took when driving the family car that were playing havoc with his wife's pulse rate. She was also bothered by the fact that he seemed to face the rest of life with the same nonchalant manner.

Two weeks in advance she would remind him that an important event was coming up that would require his taking time off from work.

"Are you sure you can get the time off?" she'd ask.

"Sure, no problem."

She'd ask him a few days later if he'd seen yet about getting the time off.

"Oh, uh . . . no, not yet, but I'm sure it won't be any problem."

Not wanting to be a nag, she'd let it go for a few days, but then she'd ask again. No, as a matter of fact, he still hadn't asked about having that time off, but he would—probably tomorrow. Only, of course tomorrow he wouldn't.

He would finally get right down to the wire, only to discover that someone else had asked for time off that day, and now the only way he could get it would be if he would go around and find someone to cover for him. That would mean a number of last-minute phone calls and conversations, and another pain or two from Diane's developing ulcer.

But instead of letting their differences drive them apart, David and Diane loved and respected each other, and vowed that they would learn from each other.

Diane worked hard at learning to take life easier when it came to the nonessentials. She had to learn not to be so obsessed about which route the couple took to the grocery store.

David had to learn that there are some things in life that are more important than deciding which fork in the road to take. He had to overcome his tendency to want to let life take him wherever it wanted to go—and for the sake of his family he began forcing himself to think about the future.

There was more than a willingness to change to get along better with the other person. There was also a recognition that the other person's attitude was often the best one to have.

Diane realized that if you spend too much time worrying about the little things, you're going to drive yourself crazy, and you're bound to take several other people with you.

David realized that if you're content just to let life take you where it will, it's probably going to take you a few places you really don't want to go.

Firstborn Male with Younger Sisters, Last-Born Female with Older Brothers

Part of the reason this combination works so well is that both partners know what to expect from members of the opposite sex. The wife has grown up feeling comfortable around males, and the husband, likewise, feels comfortable around girls and women.

To a boy there's nothing quite so good, or quite so bad, as having a little sister. She can be the ultimate pain in the neck, the snitch, the tagalong he can't get rid of. On the other hand, she is often one of the brightest spots of his existence, although he'd most certainly be the last one in the world to tell her so. She can be playful, creative, and so much fun to be around. Whatever she is, best or worst or a combination of both, her big brother does not grow up harboring very many illusions and misconceptions about women.

It's also true that for a little girl, the best and worst person in the world is likely to be her older brother.

He'll be the worst when he teases her and picks on her, sometimes so severely that he'll make her cry. It's also not much fun being the little sister when she's reached her teen years and has a crush on one of her brother's friends. The friend in question might be interested in her, too, and might even want to ask her for a date —but he probably won't ever do it because it would be too embarrassing to admit to his friend that he was interested in his friend's little sister.

Big brothers are good, though, for in spite of all the teasing they dish out, they do love their little sisters. It's often as if they're thinking, *Hey, I can pick on her because she's my sister, but I'd better not catch anyone else saying anything bad about her.* If none of big brother's friends is watching, in fact, he's probably going to treat his little sister in a fairly decent manner. He'll talk to her, share with her, give her the benefit of his extra years of experience. And in turn he will learn from her how to relate to women in general.

A marriage of the type we are discussing is more than likely going to be dominated by the male. I'm not saying that the husband won't value his wife's opinion, and seek her input in decision making and so on, but he'll be more apt to take a leadership role within his family in a loving but firm way.

His attitude won't be "Whatever you want is fine with me, dear, because I don't really care." Instead he'll be more apt to say, "Here's what I think, and what I'd like to do about the situation . . . but what do you think?" He'll have strong beliefs, but he won't force them on his wife without considering her feelings and opinion.

But in this situation the woman isn't going to be upset by that. She'll be comfortable with that arrangement because in a sense it's the same sort of relationship she always had with her big brother.

It is usually true that the woman who has grown up in a house with a big brother or two is going to enjoy the strong leadership characteristics and the authority that is built into the character of a man who has grown up looking after his little sisters.

At the same time, the man who has grown up with little sisters is likely to have a caring, loving attitude toward his wife.

The woman in this sort of marriage is going to feel very secure. And that is still an important consideration for many women, even in these modern times.

Personally, I believe that many men in our society have misunderstood what women really want from them. They think things have changed—that women are somehow not the same creatures they've always been—and that's just not true.

The man thinks that a woman doesn't want someone who's forceful and strong; that she wants a man who's sensitive and caring, and who feels very much at ease letting her be the one in charge of the relationship. And then he gets the shock of his life when he finds out the lady of his dreams has run out with a guy who has about as much sensitivity as Rambo.

I'm teasing here, of course, but just a little. Women do want men who are sensitive and caring. But they also want men who are strong enough and forceful enough to make them feel secure and protected.

She needs to know that her husband is going to be there when she needs him and that he's going to be attentive to her needs.

She wants to feel secure in the fact that he has put her first in his life and that he will work with her to build the type of home and family life that she longs for.

She also wants to feel secure financially, or to know at least that together she and her husband will move toward achieving financial security.

Again, I'm not saying that any woman wants to feel stifled or be bossed around, but she does need security and protection in the ways I've mentioned above.

I'm not suggesting, either, that a marriage involving a Firstborn male with young sisters and a Last-Born female with older brothers is going to be a brother-sister affair. Please don't think that I'm saying this is going to be a passionless, unexciting marriage. Not at all. The partners will be comfortable with each other, but their union will not be without heat and passion.

The Firstborn Male with Younger Brothers and the Last-Born Female with Older Brothers

This marriage is very similar to the one we've just discussed because the partners are happy with their roles in the marriage. If you are a Firstborn male who has grown up with younger brothers, you've probably learned to be protective of them and to be the dominant one in your family.

Meanwhile the female who has grown up with older brothers has enjoyed the protection and security their presence has brought her. She has also come to enjoy the attention that her femaleness has brought her. Not only has she had the attention that is a natural part of being the Last Born, but she has had the added attraction of being the only female in the family. This has taught her to value herself as a woman, even as she seems content to let her husband take the leadership role in the marriage.

She doesn't have to be the one in charge to know that her desires and wishes are every bit as important as her husband's. She knows very well that she's his equal as a human being, but she appreciates his desire to protect her. Please remember that the words *protect* and *stifle* are not synonymous. Again, I am not talking about some man who sees himself as lord and master of his castle and who tells his wife what to do and when to do it. No woman wants to be married to a Firstborn drill sergeant.

But then of course, if the husband really loves his wife, he's not going to treat her at all that way.

Now, if you are a Firstborn male who is contemplating marrying a Last-Born female who has older brothers, you would do well to take a look at those brothers and see what they're like. These are the people who had the dominant influence on that woman's life. If they are solid, productive people, so much the better. But if the woman has three older brothers who seem to pattern their lives after Larry, Darryl, and Darryl of *The Newhart Show,* then look out, because it's likely she's not going to think very highly of men in general.

After taking a close look at her brothers it would also be wise to look at her parents, and especially at her father. Remember that it is the opposite-sex parent who has the most influence on a child. We learn to relate to members of the opposite sex in general by the way we relate to the opposite-sex members of our immediate families.

My sister Sally, who was the oldest child in my family, had a tremendous influence on my own attitudes toward women.

Sally is loving, supportive, and caring. Even when I was at the age when I couldn't have been anything more than a pest to her, she took the time to be with me, to teach me what she knew about life, and to be my friend. In sharing her feelings with me, Sally helped me to understand the feminine perspective and to realize that boys and girls do not always see or react to the world in the same way.

From Sally I learned to appreciate the sensitivity, perceptivity, and compassion that are so much a part of the feminine makeup. I learned these things not only by observing my sister and seeing how she related to me and others but also by paying attention to her when she talked to me.

She told me what girls liked and didn't like, how they felt about things, how they wanted to be treated, and so on. Now, I must admit that when she first started talking to me about girls I thought they were all pretty yucky—except for her, of course. But a few years later I was awfully glad my sister had given me a few pointers on how to get along with the fairer sex.

I'm a rather disorganized Last Born, and my wife is a Firstborn, so we are a textbook example of a perfect-birth-order marriage. But I'd have to give my sister Sally much of the credit for giving me the skills necessary to convince a beautiful lady like Sande to marry me in the first place!

So you see that birth order in and of itself is very important, but if you want the whole picture to come into focus for you, you must consider these other influences as well.

They are a part of the overall birth-order picture.

But as a general rule, big brother, you would do very well to marry someone's little sister.

Brian has been married to Margaret for nearly ten years, and the two of them have an excellent marriage. Brian is the oldest of four children, three boys and a girl, whereas Margaret has a brother, older by some fourteen months, who was one of Brian's best friends in high school, and an older sister four years her senior.

Brian remembers that he had his eye on Margaret for quite some time, but didn't want to ask her out because he knew her big brother would make fun of him. Brian finally got his big break when Margaret's brother Tom wanted to go to a party and his parents weren't too sure they wanted him to go. They finally told him he could go, but they wanted him to take his little sister along too. Tom thought that as long as he was going to have to have her along, it would be fun to have his best friend along as well, so he asked Brian if he would do him a big favor and ask his little sister to the party.

Brian was delighted to do it, even though he tried to convince Tom he was doing him a favor of colossal proportions. They had a great time at the party and after that Brian and Margaret began dating regularly. They found that from the very start their personalities seemed to mesh perfectly.

Today, Brian says, "It's like we were born for each other. We complement each other in so many ways."

Brian didn't know a thing about birth order, or how it comes into play in a marriage, when he first started daydreaming about Margaret. But their marriage is a perfect example of how a first-and-last combination can work.

Margaret says, "God knows we're not the same. In a lot of ways our personalities are about as opposite as they can be. But that's part of the reason we get along so well."

You see, they don't butt heads, they don't step on each other's toes, and they're each content to let the other person be himself.

If you go to dinner at their house, for instance, you can be sure that Margaret is going to be doing most of the talking. That's just part of her extroverted, Last-Born nature. But Brian doesn't sit there fuming, waiting for a chance to say his piece. He enjoys listening to Margaret's good-humored conversation as much as anyone else does. He's no bump on the log when it comes to conversation, but he's perfectly content to relinquish the floor to his wife, and it does the heart good to see the loving way he looks at her from time to time while she's talking. He seems to love everything about her, including her talkative (and I do mean talkative) nature.

On the other hand, when it comes to handling the family finances, Margaret has no desire to wrest the job away from her husband. She knows that he's the organized one, and she's content to let him handle their monetary affairs. She recognizes that he is strong in this area where she is weak and is willing to act accordingly.

In every area of life they both recognize and draw from the other person's natural strengths.

They determined long ago that they would not let their obvious differences tear them apart but would instead allow those differences to bring them together.

Some people seem to run away from anyone or anything that's in the least bit different. Life is comfortable and never changing for them, but don't you imagine it must get mighty dull after a while? Can you imagine what life would be like if everyone had the same tastes you have? If everyone wanted to hear the same music, eat the same food, read the same books, and wear the same sort of clothes? It might be fun at first, and as far as I'm concerned at least I wouldn't ever have to hear any rap music or elevator melodies.

But after a while I'd start to be bored by the day-after-day sameness of it all.

The wise ones among us are those who realize that differences are capable of broadening us and teaching us more about ourselves, our world, and all the people who live in that world.

These are the people who learn from people of other cultures. They try to cultivate a taste for different kinds of food, music, et cetera.

And this is how Brian and Margaret approached their marriage. They would welcome the differences in each other and try to learn from them, rather than attempting to mold each other into carbon copies.

I'm not suggesting that you have to enjoy and appreciate everything about your partner that's different from you. There are some things you'd do well to eliminate.

I heard about a man, for instance, who was a missionary to a remote part of Africa. One of the things he wanted to be careful to do was to accept the customs of the people. He certainly didn't want to offend them, because then they wouldn't listen to him when he preached.

On one occasion he was particularly nervous, because the village leaders had called for a feast in his honor. He knew the people ate many foods that would be difficult for the stomach of an American to digest, and he had no idea what delicacy they might set before him on this occasion.

As he sat at the table with the important men of the village, he was pleased to discover that a barbecue pit had been dug for the occasion, and a couple of fat pigs were being made ready. He figured that would be just fine. He wasn't going to raise a ruckus about barbecued pork, even if he didn't have any hickory-flavored sauce to go with it.

As the platters of meat were brought in he began to relax even more. It looked good, and it smelled good too.

But then the feast took an unexpected turn. A special plate was brought in, prepared especially for the guest of honor, and set before him. It was piled high, with steaming hot . . . pig intestines.

It seems that in this particular village the intestines were considered the very best part. People usually sought after them the way a couple of American kids would argue over who got the wishbone from a chicken.

But because he was the guest of honor, the people of the village had done him the ultimate kindness and presented him with a pound and a half of their favorite food.

"I don't know how I got them down," the missionary said. "But I did."

I don't know how you feel about it, but my hat goes off to that fellow. I've eaten a few "exotic" foods in my life, but I would never, ever, chomp down on a pig's intestine, no matter how many people were going to be offended if I didn't!

My purpose here isn't to gross you out talking about pig intestines. I use the story as an illustration merely to suggest that some people are different from me in ways that are good and that would broaden my horizons and enable me to handle some situations better. There are other differences that are not good, and that I do not need to accept.

For instance, if I am the type who falls to pieces whenever I'm under the least bit of pressure, and yet my partner remains cool and calm and thus accomplishes much more in that situation than I could ever hope to, I can say, "I liked the way you handled that situation. How can you remain so calm when everything is getting so crazy?"

It would be absolutely crazy if the other partner said, "Hey, I really liked the way you went all to pieces and made a bad situation even worse. Show me how to do that so I can behave that way next time."

You see, a First-Last marriage like Brian and Margaret's works so well because they have learned how their strengths and weaknesses mesh together, and they have learned to concentrate on the strengths instead of the weaknesses. Together, complementing each other, allowing each to be strong where he is strong, they have a nearly perfect marriage.

I say nearly, because I don't believe any marriage is truly perfect. Well, since Sande might be reading this, I suppose I ought to rephrase that. There is no marriage that doesn't have occasional misunderstandings, arguments, and moments of tension. Those things are going to occur in any relationship between two intelligent human beings. If you're looking at your friends' marriage wondering why it's so much better than yours, stop worrying about it right now, because you don't have the slightest idea what really goes on in their house when they're alone behind closed doors.

The Firstborn Male with Sisters and the Last-Born Female with Brothers

It ought to be obvious why this marriage is going to be such a solid success. This has all of the elements. First of all it's a First-Last combination. And then the husband will have grown up around sisters, so he is comfortable with women. He is going to respect his wife, understand something about her psychological makeup as a female, and probably be a caring, supportive husband. The wife, meanwhile, grew up in a home where there were boys in the family, so she understands what makes the male of the species tick.

Furthermore, this Firstborn male will most likely be comfortably able to assume the leadership role in the home. He won't shirk his responsibilities toward his wife and children when it comes to finances, discipline, or any other part of family life. And his Last-Born spouse will be able to let him be the "head of the house" without suffering any damage to her ego.

I'm not saying that a marriage such as this one is a surefire success story. But because it has so many of the proper elements going for it, you have to work pretty hard at it if you want to make a failure out of it.

If you're a single Firstborn male who has younger sisters, let me give you a little piece of advice. The next time you're at a party and see a pretty woman, don't ask her what sign she is. Do something more original and more worthwhile, and ask her about her birth order. If she tells you she's the last in her family, ask her if she happens to have an older brother or two. If she does, hurry up and ask her out before somebody else beats you to it.

When it comes to the perfect romantic partner, she's probably going to be just what the Doctor (Leman) ordered for you. Chances are good that the two of you will be quite compatible and comfortable together—although I would also suggest that you get to know her a little bit better before asking her to marry you.

But now I'm sure that someone is going to ask the obvious questions: If Firstborns and Last Borns are so good together, where does that leave the Middle Borns—out in the cold? Am I suggesting that Middle Borns should just remain single? The answer to that is of course not.

A Firstborn–Middle-Born combination can be an excellent match—but it can also be an extremely poor match. Which it is depends more upon the Middle Born than the Firstborn—and if you want to know more about that, turn to the section titled "For Middle Borns Only." First, though, I want to tell you about some

THE MARRIAGE MILEAGE CHART

	FIRSTBORN	MIDDLE BORN	LAST BORN
FIRSTBORN	This combination is likely to resemble an Olympic competition more than a marriage. Two Firstborns will either be butting heads from day one—or they will be involved in a controller-pleaser relationship.	The problems with this combination is that the Middle Born may modify his own behavior to please his Firstborn mate. But remember that Middle Borns are generally more successful when it comes to building lasting marriages than are the other birth orders.	Firstborn–Last Born is an excellent combination. Firstborn can teach Last Born how to be better organized, and that there are times when life must be taken seriously.
MIDDLE BORN	Married to a hard-driving Firstborn, the Middle Born may be inclined to give up his own desires and dreams to please his Firstborn spouse. If the Middle Born has some Last-Born tendencies, this marriage can work well.	This combination can work well if one of the Middle Borns has Firstborn tendencies and the other has Last-Born traits. Otherwise, this marriage may be suffocated by too much compromise.	In the Middle-Born–Last-Born combination the Middle Born may find himself being pulled into an "irresponsible" life-style. This combination works better if the Middle Born has some Firstborn tendencies.
LAST BORN	Last Born–Firstborn is an excellent combination. The Last Born teaches the Firstborn that it's okay to have fun once in a while.	Again, this combination will work well if the Middle Born leans more in the direction of being a Firstborn than he does toward being a Last Born.	Watch out for this combination. Sure, you'll have fun, but you may find that life gets out of control every once in a while. Who's in charge here?

particular mistakes that Firstborns make—especially Firstborn females—during the search for a lifetime partner.

That's coming up next.

Things Last Borns Can Teach Firstborns

—To stop and take it easy every once in a while

—That laughter can be a wonderful thing

—The fine art of selling yourself

—That it's not going to kill you to throw caution to the winds every once in a while

—That it's not a sign of weakness to be loving and affectionate

—That there isn't anybody anywhere who doesn't goof up at one time or another, and that it's better to laugh at your mistakes than to cry over them

—That the tortoise may have won the race, but he sure didn't have as much fun as the hare did!

Celebrity Couples and Birth Order

Now, before moving on, let's take a look at how birth order may be influencing some of the famous romances of our era, according to *Cosmopolitan* magazine.[3]

PRINCE CHARLES AND PRINCESS DIANA: *Cosmopolitan* says that the prince's personality reflects his position as the oldest brother of mostly boys: "a leader who likes to be in charge, a meticulous person, bordering on perfectionistic, who expects a lot from his wife." Princess Diana, on the other hand, is a youngest girl who also has one younger brother. The magazine's conclusions?

"Charles and Diana are relatively well matched, but her playfulness and Charles's benign disapproval of it are predictable."

THE DUKE AND DUCHESS OF YORK: Prince Andrew is a Middle Born, while Fergie is the youngest of two daughters. This match gets a hearty nod of approval.

RONALD AND NANCY REAGAN: The former President is the younger of two boys, while Nancy is an Only Child. This may not be the very best matchup in the history of Birth Order, but these two know how to make their marriage work. *Cosmopolitan* quotes the former President as saying, "We're happy! . . . We talk about everything. . . . I always feel better knowing that we're in agreement."

TATUM O'NEAL AND JOHN McENROE: Uh-oh. Two Firstborns here. Both Mr. and Mrs. McEnroe have two younger brothers, and that may be the saving grace of this matchup—since Tatum grew up dealing with members of the male species. She is also four years younger than her husband, so she may be more willing to follow his lead than she would be if they were the same age. This marriage, like any marriage consisting of two Firstborns, is going to need plenty of tender loving care.

4

The Firstborn Detective in Search of a Partner

Going on a date, or to a party?

Are you ready to go?

Let's see. Yes, every hair is in place. Your new outfit looks perfect. You've used a powerful shampoo to make sure you don't have dandruff, a toothpaste that's guaranteed to leave your teeth so white, they'll blind anyone who sees you smile, and that cologne is just the right combination of seduction and mystery.

But wait a minute. Have you done your homework?

Someone says, "Homework? What homework?"

Why, your private-eye homework, of course.

Before you go on that date, or head off to that party where many potential dates might be found, you need a quick course in how to be a romantic detective.

A romantic detective is someone who can spot the difference between Mr. Right and Mr. Wrong at fifty paces. She knows what her own personality traits are, and she also knows how to spot the personality traits that are best going to complement her. She knows the sort of person she should run toward, as well as the sort of person she should run *from!*

Does the idea of being a romantic detective bother you? It shouldn't. I know, I know. . . . I've heard all the things people say about love: "Love is blind," and "I couldn't help myself," and "I fell in love at first sight." At the risk of being branded an unromantic cynic, I want to tell you what I think about all of those statements:

Bullcrumble!

The truth is that nobody should enter into a romantic relationship unless he has his eyes wide open. Love—especially the sort of love that's going to result in a lifetime commitment between two people—is much too important to be left to chance. I am not saying here that you find someone who meets all of your exacting standards and then decide to fall in love with him. Love doesn't work that way. But neither should you allow yourself to be swept into a relationship with someone who—if you looked at him in the cold, analytical light of day—doesn't have any of the qualities you need in a lover.

You might be attracted to a person like that. But then, after giving the situation a good second and third look, you'd be wise to put the brakes on. Remember, you're the one in control of your life and your heart, and you should see that it stays that way.

I remember seeing James Brown, the Godfather of Soul himself, on *American Bandstand*—must be nearly twenty-five years ago now. (Can you believe that Dick Clark used to be about fifteen years older than I am, then for a while we were the same age, and now he's younger than I am!)

Anyway, James Brown was singing, "I'm just a prisoner! I'm just a prisoner! I'm just a prisoner of love!" While he sang, the man gave every appearance of being in agony. Sweat dripped down his forehead, his mouth was twisted into an expression of excruciating pain. I wanted to yell at him, "No! No! You're not just a prisoner! Nobody has to be a prisoner of love! Especially not a love that isn't good for you!"

I know that for most single people—men and women—there comes a time when thoughts turn to finding someone with whom to share a lifetime, settling down and (perhaps) raising a family.

Whether that time has arrived for you, or whether you are just looking for someone with whom to establish a steady dating relationship, there are certain things that you, as a Firstborn, must be aware of as you look for a potential partner.

In Chapter Three I told you why the best partner for you is more than likely going to be a Last Born, and pointed out some of the reasons why that is true. Now I'm going to turn things around a bit and tell who you shouldn't pick for your partner.

Five Things Not to Look for in a Mate

1. Don't marry someone just because you're reminded of Mommy or Daddy.
2. Don't marry someone just because that person's not at all like Mommy or Daddy.
3. Don't think that a person will make good marriage material just because he's someone you can compete with.
4. Don't be fooled by appearances.
5. Don't be blinded by money, status, or position.

Let me explain:

1. DON'T MARRY SOMEONE BECAUSE YOU'RE REMINDED OF MOMMY OR DADDY

The Firstborn romantic detective needs to be especially on the lookout for this one. If he's earned his private investigator's credentials, he's going to know how to spot the early warning signs and avoid hooking up with someone who's merely a replacement for Mater or Pater.

This is one of the most common mistakes Firstborns make, and women more often than men. It's crazy, but true, that women who didn't particularly care for their fathers, and who couldn't wait to grow up and get married so they could get away from their fathers, very often wind up marrying men who are just like their fathers!

Now, if your father is a wonderful human being, if he always treated your mother with loving respect, and if he was always there for you when you were a little girl, then more power to you. Find a man like that, and you'll be doing very well indeed. What I am talking about here, though, is women who become involved with men who are going to be eternally critical and impossible to please—just like Daddy was—or men who find themselves involved with women who are going to treat them like their mothers did. Too many men seem to be looking for a substitute for Mom, when they really ought to be looking for a wife.

We talked about this sort of situation briefly when we discussed marriage between two Firstborns. Remember Janet, who traded domination by her father for domination by her husband?

I have seen that sort of thing happen over and over again. I don't think any woman goes and purposefully seeks out a man who is going to push her around. But if she has been pushed around and belittled all her life, she may begin to think that this is what she deserves. More than likely she won't believe you if you tell her that's what she's doing, because it's not a conscious choice. But subconsciously there's no doubt about it.

Her life-style orients her toward rejection and abuse at the hands of the males in her life. You see, every human being follows a particular life-style. His life-style may not be what he thinks his life is about, or what he says he's after, but it is the way he has been trained to live his life.

The concept of life-style was developed by the pioneer psychologist Alfred Adler and it means, basically, that everything we do is oriented toward some goal—good or bad—whether or not we ourselves know what that goal is.[1] Adler also said that a life-style is formed very early in life, and will generally be followed throughout the rest of a person's life unless he comes to understand what he is doing and takes specific steps to change things.

I think about Rita, who, while talking about the things her

husband did to make her feel stupid and worthless, would pause every once in a while and say, "But I'm so lucky to have him."

Rita was an attractive woman. Beyond that she was intelligent, articulate, and had a good sense of humor.

When pressed for the reason she kept saying she was "so lucky" to have her husband, she said, "Well, if he hadn't come along, I probably never would have gotten married."

"Why in the world do you think that?" I asked.

"Well . . ." She thought for a moment. "Who else would have me?"

My own impression was that she never would have married Bruce—or put up with his abuse for so many years—if her self-esteem hadn't been practically nonexistent in the first place.

Some women never do a single thing to please their fathers, but they never give up trying. They marry men who are just like not-so-dear old Dad, because if they can finally do something to please their husbands it's going to be like gaining approval from Dad. How sad, though, that many perfectly capable, fine women spend their whole lives trying to please unappreciative men who wouldn't be impressed by any woman from Joan of Arc to Venus de Milo.

No woman deserves to be mistreated at the hands of any man. If the man you're interested in marrying doesn't treat you with the utmost gentleness and respect, "dump the chump." I'm not saying he has to run before you everywhere you go, throwing rose petals in your path, or that he has to put his cloak across mud puddles for you—but he had better respect and appreciate you as a human being.

Did your father always treat you as if you were Daddy's help-less little girl? Ask yourself if you'd like to receive the same sort of treatment from the man in your life. You deserve to be your mate's equal partner, not his silly little cutie pie.

Was it hard to get your dad to take your views seriously? What about the man in your life? Does he think you're being cute or silly when you're dead serious? Does he refuse to get involved in a serious discussion with you because "you just wouldn't understand these things"? Yikes! Chuck the relationship out the nearest window.

Was your father domineering and hard to please? Take a long, hard look at the man you're seeing and make sure you're not going to spend your life trying to please Daddy.

2. DON'T MARRY SOMEONE JUST BECAUSE THAT PERSON ISN'T AT ALL LIKE MOMMY OR DADDY

This is another common mistake Firstborns make. Women are so tired of being pushed around by their fathers that they "fall in love" with men they can easily dominate and control. Or men are so resentful at what they perceived as their mothers' weak behavior that they pick women who are going to push them around and make their lives miserable. There could be many reasons for not wanting to marry someone who reminds you of your mother or father but not one of them, in and of itself, is reason enough for marrying someone.

A problem for the woman who becomes romantically involved with a weak man simply because he is not at all like her father, is that a woman will not respect a man she can easily control and the marriage is not likely to be a happy one.

When there is no mutual respect, no give-and-take, there is not going to be excitement and growth. Instead there is bound to be stagnation and dissatisfaction.

All of her life Theresa had been put down and made to feel worthless by her father. Dad had come to this country from his native Italy—which he referred to as "the Old Country"—and as far as his daughter was concerned, his attitudes about women should have been left in an old country. There was certainly nothing new or enlightened about them.

Her father saw women as little more than decorations. God meant them to be beautiful, but not intelligent.

> NO WOMAN DESERVES TO BE MISTREATED AT
> THE HANDS OF ANY MAN. IF THE MAN YOU'RE
> INTERESTED IN MARRYING DOESN'T TREAT YOU
> WITH THE UTMOST GENTLENESS AND RESPECT,
> DUMP THE CHUMP.

They were good for looking at, but not for listening to.

Theresa's mother put up with his condescension toward her and even seemed to support him in his attitudes. In fact, she tried to teach her daughter that a woman should never try to compete in a man's world. That wasn't the way God expected women to behave.

Theresa received good grades in school, but her father never seemed to care. But it was a totally different story where her brother was concerned. Her father couldn't say enough about anything Joseph did. Joseph was encouraged to excel, and money was put into an account so he could attend a good college.

Theresa, on the other hand, was expected to find a good husband and spend her life cooking, cleaning, and having babies.

As Theresa entered her teen years, the anger within her reached the boiling point. She watched her mother sit at home every night while her father went out to have a good time with the boys or—more likely—with the girls. She had no proof, but she felt certain that her father was seeing other women. It certainly wouldn't have surprised her. It would merely be more evidence of his archaic views about women in general.

Still, Mama sat at home, working on her knitting, keeping the house clean, and doing everything else a woman was supposed to do. Theresa vowed she would never be like her mother, nor would she ever allow a man to treat her this way.

To express her anger, she began rebelling in conventional ways. She shocked her father by coming home drunk. It had been expected when Joseph did the same thing, but it was a disgrace for a young woman to behave in such a fashion. She began smoking too —not just cigarettes—and dating many different men. Her motto could have been What's good for the goose is good for the gander, but what she didn't realize is that What's bad for the goose is bad for the gander, because her hedonistic life-style nearly destroyed her.

Finally, when she overcame her drinking, her drugs, and her wild living, she decided it was time to settle down.

Her first priority was to find a man who was willing to let her be fulfilled as a person. She was going to live her life the way she wanted to live it, and no man was going to stand in her way!

I'm not sure where she met her husband, but he was from a nice family and I believe his surname was Milquetoast. Even though he wasn't of Italian descent, I'm quite sure he was using a piece of spaghetti as a backbone. At least that's the way it seemed when it came to Theresa.

You've heard of people who are so dominated that all you have to say to them is "Jump," and they'll ask, "How high?" Well, this poor fellow was so busy jumping that his feet hardly ever touched the ground.

There wasn't anything he wouldn't do for Theresa. He was, oh, so proud of her and supported her in everything she did. If she wanted to spend their money to take a ski trip with some of her friends, that was fine. If she wanted him to stay home with the baby while she took an evening art class, that was wonderful too.

The more he gave in, the more demanding she became, and the more he would smile and tell her he loved her.

Was she happy?

Absolutely not! She was miserable. Maybe it was better than the way her father had treated her all those years, but then again, maybe it wasn't. Both situations left her unfulfilled and frustrated.

Theresa was learning that a marriage is an equal partnership. She realized that a husband and wife are meant to work together and make decisions together, and she was awfully tired of always having the upper hand.

Well, you can imagine how poor Caspar felt when his wife told him she was unhappy in their marriage and wanted to go for counseling. The poor guy had done everything Theresa had ever wanted him to do. What more could he do to make her happy? He was trying to be sensitive, and not too macho. As a matter of fact, he seemed intent on patterning his own behavior after two of his heroes from the silver screen: Woody Allen and Alan Alda.

It wasn't easy to convince him that he had to throw in a little bit of Sylvester Stallone and Clint Eastwood as well. Finally, though, after much practice and some concentrated effort, he started standing up to Theresa every once in a while.

She wasn't happy when he wouldn't let her push him around, and she did some yelling. But deep down she was happy that he was demonstrating some backbone, and she was happier with her marriage. As a matter of fact so was her husband.

There are many women who make the mistake Theresa made. They think they want to find men who aren't anything at all like their fathers, and they bend so far to avoid doing that that they become involved with men who are just as irritating as Dad was, but in the opposite direction.

For example:

If Dad or Mom was a workaholic, be careful that you're not attracted to someone just because of his fun-loving, I-don't-have-a-care-in-the-world attitude.

If Dad was rigid, legalistic, and perfectionistic, be sure that gentleman you're attracted to has more going for him than his tendency to be a rebel.

If Mom tended to smother you with her affection, you might have the key as to why you're so desperately attracted to a woman who seems indifferent to you.

If your opposite-sex parent had the backbone of an amoeba, you may be attracted to someone who is forceful and authoritative, whether or not there's anything else about him that would attract you.

If Mom or Dad was extremely religious, you may be fascinated by and drawn to someone who is openly rebellious against conventional religion.

Of course, all of these situations could be true in reverse too.

Whatever your father did to you, however the man may have failed as a parent, should have absolutely no bearing on what you look for in a husband. Keep reminding yourself that you are looking for a partner, and not someone to replace your father or to be the father you never had.

3. DON'T THINK THAT SOMEONE WILL MAKE GOOD MARRIAGE MATERIAL JUST BECAUSE THEY'RE SOMEONE YOU CAN COMPETE WITH

You're a Firstborn romantic detective, out for a first date with a good-looking guy (or girl). As the evening goes on, you begin to think that maybe he's just a little bit too good looking. I mean, how much time did he spend on that hair anyway?

And then, over dinner, you notice that he seems to be playing some one-upmanship games. You're competitive by nature yourself, and so you're rather enjoying this. The whole thing is creating some sparks, and if you weren't such a good romantic detective you might even mistake it for chemistry.

One thing you need to keep very firmly in mind: There is a healthy degree of competition in most any relationship. But competition is one thing. War is something else!

Maybe it sounds silly, but many Firstborns make the mistake of thinking that marriage is a track meet. They may not realize it, but deep down inside they view the marriage relationship as a lifelong competition.

A woman may say, "I want a man who'll challenge me, and strengthen me, and bring out the best in me." And I can respect that, unless what she really means is "Bring him on, I'll take him. I'm up for the battle."

The man, meanwhile, is apt to be thinking, *I'm not going to let any woman show* me *up!* Most men, you see, have a bit of the chauvinist within them—probably even Alan Alda.

When it comes to a male-female partnership, mutual respect is one thing—but mutual competition is something entirely different. This is one of the reasons so many aggressive Firstborns wind up married to aggressive Firstborns; but a marriage in which the husband and wife have the continual desire to get the best of each other will end in failure.

There is an initial excitement that brings such people together. They both have the same attitude about life. They're both winners and think they ought to team up. Only, there isn't any teamwork on this team. Every now and then a wife needs her husband to forget about his own needs and desires and give her a boost. And, in the same way, a husband occasionally needs his wife to forget about herself and give him the encouragement he needs.

But if you're looking at marriage as a track meet, the only objective is to cross the finish line first, and you have no time to stop and help your spouse. Having a little bit of competition in a marriage is fine and may even be healthy. But having too much, or having that competition be the driving force behind the marriage, means you're likely to be headed for an appearance on *Divorce Court.*

4. DON'T BE FOOLED BY APPEARANCES

I hate to have to even mention this. But the truth of the matter is that we human beings put a great deal of emphasis on physical appearance. I really don't think women are quite as guilty of this as men are.

Men make the mistake of thinking that a woman with a great pair of legs also has a terrific personality—but it ain't necessarily so. I tell men to be careful not to confuse their libidos with their hearts.

But no matter how much I might warn against doing so, it's still true that most of us seem to think we can see into a person's character by the way he looks—and that is absolutely not true.

How many times have you seen an article about a con man who cheated some elderly woman out of her life's savings?

The woman says, "But he seemed like such a nice young man. He had such an honest face!"

You cannot read a person's character, or the content of his heart, simply by looking at his face, or into his eyes.

It steams me that we place such an emphasis on physical appearance. Part of this is due to the messages that bombard us every day, compliments of the folks on Madison Avenue.

The people who write the TV commercials we see seem to stress the notion that it's the superficial things that are important. I don't begrudge what they're doing. I understand that they're trying to sell their clients' products, but I wish they could find a better way to do it. No one is going to sell me anything by telling me that I'm worthless unless I use the right shampoo, toothpaste, makeup, deodorant, or wear clothes from the right designer. I think more highly of myself than that.

Unfortunately, though, there are thousands and perhaps millions of people who do believe it—and who compare themselves to the beautiful models they see on TV. And that applies to men and women.

If you're concentrating on your own externals and neglecting what's inside, then you're only fooling yourself about what kind of person you are. If you're concentrating on the externals when it comes to selecting a mate, then you're concentrating on the unimportant matters.

A few years back a rock group by the name of The Police had a hit record with the lyric "We are spirits/In the material world."

Well, because we do live in the material world, the first thing we are going to notice about another person, especially an opposite-sex person, is his or her appearance.

But ask yourself whether this good-looking guy is as attractive over the telephone as he is in person.

Does she seem so wonderful when you're not staring into those deep blue (or green, or brown) eyes?

Are you still going to love him when he's got a big round bald spot right on the top of his head?

Will she still set your heart aflame when she has to wear support hose to conceal her varicose veins?

Not long ago, when I was on the road, I stepped into an ice-cream parlor to indulge myself in a double dipper. The young woman behind the counter seemed like a very pleasant person. She had a delightful sense of humor and the sort of smile that made you just have to smile back at her. There weren't any other customers waiting, so after I paid for my ice cream I stood and talked to her for a while. Then, as I left, she told me that she hoped I'd enjoy my stay in her town and wished me a pleasant evening.

As I walked around the corner I looked back through the shop's window and saw her engaged in a pleasant conversation with another customer.

I had two thoughts:

1. What a sweetheart!
2. What a pity!

What did I mean by that? Well, this woman, who seemed so pleasant, so bright, and so concerned about others, was also about seventy-five pounds overweight. She didn't have a double chin. Hers was a triple chin, and she had a long, crooked nose. I'm not saying all this to be cruel. I'm telling you the truth.

And I knew that it was highly unlikely that any young men her age would be burning up her phone lines or vying to be the first one on her dance card.

No, they'd be out chasing the 35-24-35 with the silky hair and the big blue eyes, even if the glamor girl didn't have a thing to offer besides her appearance. How I wish God had made us so that we could see each other's character with our eyes, but He just didn't do it that way. I'm not suggesting that a person can't be attractive and also have a railroad-carful of other good attributes, but I am saying that physical attraction is not a sufficient foundation on which to build a lasting marriage.

A few years ago the sitcom *Cheers,* had an episode in which

Diane Chambers was going to prove that she was not a snob who based her romantic relationships on the man's appearance. She would do this by dating a man who was not particularly attractive.

She dated the man several times and discovered that he was everything she could possibly want. He was witty, intelligent, and he shared a number of interests with her.

But in the final moments of the show she broke down and confessed that she had broken up with him for the simple reason that she did not find him physically attractive. She cried and carried on and admitted that she hated herself for being so hung up on appearances, but she simply couldn't help it.

That show made, in a very funny way, the point I'm trying to make. There is much, much more to a man than the way he looks. If you find a man who is caring, supportive, sensitive to your needs, one who has a stimulating personality, a good sense of humor, and if you have some things in common—then don't be overly concerned about it if he looks more like Alfred E. Neuman than he does Paul Newman!

I recently went to see a dermatologist because I was having some problems with the skin around my nose. He didn't make me feel any better when he told me that I have a condition called rosacea, and that I will continue to have it for the rest of my life.

Rosacea is the same thing W. C. Fields had, and it causes the nose to become red and bulbous. I have just the beginnings of the disease, but even as the dermatologist was telling me about it, I had visions of myself spending the rest of my life looking like an advertisement for the folks at Ringling Bros.

I was very discouraged and depressed when I told my wife, Sande, what I had found out.

But her reaction cheered me up. She said, "Well, it's not really any big deal. I love you just the way you are!"

Now, she could have said, "Well, don't worry—we'll go to a plastic surgeon and have it fixed." Or she could have said, "Gee— I hope it won't look too bad!"

But her reaction, instead, was to reassure me that her love for me wasn't dependent upon my appearance. You see, a quality person is able to overlook physical blemishes and flaws and concentrate on what's inside!

5. DON'T BE BLINDED BY MONEY, STATUS, OR POSITION

So somebody says, "Listen, Doc, who do you think I am? You must think I'm incredibly selfish. First you tell me not to fall for some guy just because he's nice looking, and now you tell me not to be blinded by money, status, or position. Come on, give me some credit."

Right.

There may be a few people on the face of this planet who couldn't be blinded by any amount of money, status, or position, but I doubt if there are too many of them. The gospel truth is that we human beings are creatures who have a great deal of trouble seeing anything else when we get a couple of great big dollar signs in our eyes.

I can still hear Frankie Valli and the Four Seasons singing to a lovely young lady named Dawn: "Think what a big man he'll be, Think of the places you'll see; Now think what the future would be with a poor boy like me. Dawn, go away, please go away!" I can just see the boy's eyes getting as big as saucers when Dawn says, "You know, you're right. I have thought about it and I'd be a fool to throw my future away on the likes of you."

If you're a romantic, you know that's just what the lady in question was going to do. She'd tell her penniless lover that she didn't care about money anyway. It was love that was important, and they'd work hard to build a future together.

But if, on the other hand, you're a hard-headed realist, you figure that the girl wrote the pros and cons of marrying the poor guy on separate sides of a piece of paper—and was in church saying "I do" to the rich guy the very next week!

I am kidding, of course. But our society puts so much emphasis on money and status that it's hard not to get swept up in the worship of such things.

Have you ever had anybody tell you that money can't buy happiness, and you wondered what they'd been smoking lately? Well, let me tell you that it's true—money can't buy happiness, especially when it comes to marriage.

If you ever tell yourself, "I'm not sure I love him, but he'll take very good care of me," or if financial security becomes your overriding concern, it's time to stop, step back, and take stock of the relationship.

In my private practice I counsel people from all different professions, races, religions, and from all layers of the social strata. But I am never surprised to see someone in my office who I know to have a fat bank account, a beautiful house, and an expensive car or two. I never have said to anyone, "Hey, what are you doing here? You're rich!"

I would go so far as to say that most of the married couples who come to me for counseling are fairly well off financially. They're successful, but they're not deliriously happy. Happiness comes from love, respect, and compatibility, and not from having plenty of money or having people look up to you.

How can you tell if you're really attracted to his money instead of just to him?

—Instead of going to a fancy restaurant, take some peanut-butter-and-jelly sandwiches to the park and see how much fun you have.

—Spend a few evenings together without spending any money—going for a walk, watching an old movie on TV, swinging in the park, et cetera—and see if he's as exciting when he doesn't touch his wallet.

—Take a good, long look at that expensive suit, and then at the person wearing it, and honestly decide which one you like better.

Before we move on, I want to mention three other mistakes that are usually the exclusive territory of Firstborn men. Guys, be sure to see that you:

1. Don't look for a woman who is going to baby and pamper you. (Stay home with Mom and save the attorney's fees!)
2. Don't mistake your ladylove for the maid.
3. Don't confuse a relationship with a rescue operation.

Let's take these one at a time:

1. DON'T LOOK FOR A WOMAN WHO IS GOING TO BABY YOU

This is a lot like marrying a woman because she reminds you of your mother. The main difference, though, is that this man is specifically looking for someone who is going to coddle him. First-born males in particular may do this because they were always so close to their mothers—and remember, the most important parent in a person's life is his opposite-sex parent.

When you were little and you fell down and got a boo-boo, who did you want to kiss it and make it well? Mom, of course.

When you had the flu and had to stay in bed, who would come in and rub your back, tousle your hair, and make you feel better? Again, it was good old Mom.

Who was it who agreed to work in the concession stand at your Little League game, bake cookies for your class party, and go on the field trip with your fourth-grade class? You got it. Mom!

I'm not naive enough to think that every man grew up in a home with a mother like that. Not every Mom in the world is patterned after Margaret Anderson on *Father Knows Best* or June Cleaver on *Leave It to Beaver.*

But there are a great many men who have had selfless, always-giving Moms like the ones I've been describing above. And, naturally, those men are going to expect the same sort of behavior from their wives that they got from their mothers.

One man said, "When I was a kid, my mother did everything for me. She went without things so I could have them, and I never appreciated it very much. I remember, for instance, if we were having fried chicken for dinner, she'd let me have one of the breasts, while she'd eat a couple of wings or drumsticks. I just figured that was the way mothers were supposed to be. In fact I didn't have any sisters, so I suppose I figured that's the way women in general were supposed to act. It was just natural for them to do without and to always be thinking of others ahead of themselves."

He hadn't been married very long when he got over that notion.

"The first time my wife and I had an argument, it was a big shock to me. We were getting ready to go out for the evening, and I wanted to see a particular movie. It wasn't something my wife was interested in.

"She told me, at first, that she'd rather see something else. I replied that I was sorry about that, but I was really looking forward to seeing this movie. She informed me in no uncertain terms that she didn't want to see it at all, and if I wanted to see it so badly, I could go all by myself."

He was shocked at what he considered his wife's selfishness.

"I told her I couldn't believe she could be so self-centered, and she told me that I was the one who always had to have my way."

He stormed out of the house and did as his wife had suggested —attending the movie by himself.

But he didn't enjoy it at all, because as soon as the opening credits were rolling, he realized that what his wife had said was absolutely correct. He was the one who always decided where they were going to go and what they were going to do. No way in the world had he been treating her as his equal partner. He had been expecting her to cater to his every whim, to make her own feelings and desires subordinate to his.

His mother had been a wonderful human being, but she had left him with the impression that all women enjoyed being martyrs who poured themselves out in service to others. Sitting in that theater, he realized that he had been expecting way too much from his wife, and that his view of women had been completely distorted. He had seen them as ethereal, angelic, altruistic creatures instead of flesh-and-blood human beings.

He immediately left the theater, went home, and apologized to his wife for his behavior. From that point on their marriage was better than it had been before.

Every man—and especially the Firstborn—needs to remember that the woman he chooses to marry is going to be his wife and not his mother. It is not her duty to take care of him, to see to it that he's smart enough to wear his galoshes when it rains, nor should she be expected to drop everything she's doing to wait on him if he's got a cold or the flu.

Because your wife loves you, she will want to do things for you. She will want to nurture you when you're ill, for instance, but she is doing it out of her love for you and not because it is her duty.

And remember that turnabout is fair play.

If your wife pampers and looks after you when you've got the flu, you ought to do the same for her when she is ill.

If she is the sort of person who will do things you want to do, even though she's not particularly crazy about them, then you should do some things she wants to do that may not be your usual cup of tea.

Whatever loving, caring things she does for you, do them right back to her.

Stephen and Meg Hectus, of Mentor, Ohio, are a husband and wife who know what partnership and teamwork are all about.

For four years Meg suffered from a "superinfection" that made it difficult for her to breathe. She required surgery and extensive medication. She told the *USA Today* newspaper that Stephen helped her find her way through the most difficult of those times:

"Stephen can make me laugh on the way to the emergency room by responding to my 'I don't want you to be upset if I die,' with, 'Meg, you're not going to die! You have a good ten, maybe fifteen years of suffering ahead of you!'

"He has learned to set up IVs, change dressings, and ready Adrenalin shots. He brings dinner—table, chairs, candles, and all —up to our bedroom for a weekend family get-together when I am too weak to come downstairs. Incredibly, he walks in smiling every evening and will rub my back for hours when I can't sleep.

. . . Stephen escorts me to a wedding, and I feel glamorous and not swollen from cortisone.

"Being a hero is not always easy and sometimes Stephen cries. That gives me the opportunity of comforting him for a change, and I feel needed."[2]

This couple obviously knows what love and marriage are all about.

2. DON'T MISTAKE YOUR LADYLOVE FOR THE MAID

Another big problem for Firstborn men.

This may be related to seeing a lover as a mother figure, but it's also rooted in a misunderstanding of the roles of the sexes.

Some men believe that women are meant to be neat and tidy, while God didn't design a male brain that knows where the dirty-clothes hamper is.

Well, it just ain't so.

A friend told me recently, "I always thought girls were neat, clean, creatures, while boys went around with dirt on their faces and made messes everywhere they went. But that was before I had a daughter."

He described his ten-year-old daughter's bedroom by saying, "Daniel Boone would probably be afraid to go in there."

The girl cleaned her room once a week, but the rest of the time it resembled Berlin immediately after World War II. Meanwhile his two sons' rooms were relatively orderly and neat.

There is nothing in the makeup of the female that relegates her to the role of cleaner-upper or organizer. Nor is there anything in her makeup that says that she should be content to follow you around picking up after you.

She should not be expected to wait on you when you're perfectly capable of doing things for yourself.

You may be thinking that you don't expect your sweetheart to serve as your maid, but here's a little quiz to see if that's really true:

1. When you take a bath or shower, do you always make sure the bathroom is straightened up afterward?
2. When you and your wife are sitting at home together and the telephone rings, which one of you is expected to answer it?
3. You and your wife are watching your favorite television show, and you suddenly become very thirsty. Do you go into the kitchen and get yourself a drink, or do you ask your wife to get one for you? And, if you do get up for yourself, do you ask your wife if she'd like you to bring her something?
4. Do you hang your coat up, put your shoes in the closet, and your dirty clothes in the hamper, or do you just leave them wherever they happen to fall?
5. You wake up in the middle of the night feeling hungry. After you go into the kitchen and make yourself a snack, are you careful to clean up after yourself?
6. You wake up in the middle of the night feeling hungry. Do you wake your wife and ask her if she'll go into the kitchen and fix you a snack?
7. After supper, when it's time to clear the dishes from the table and clean up, do you help your wife or do you expect her to do it herself, while you sit and read the newspaper?
8. Do you ever help your wife with the household chores?

Okay, now that you've taken the quiz, I'm going to let you off the hook. I'm not going to tell you how to score it, because that should be obvious. Perhaps you can look back over all these questions and see that you don't really expect your wife to be your maid. Or, you see that you do treat your wife as a maid in many ways, although you may not have realized it before.

If you are guilty, I would urge you to do your best to change your ways. You can start out by talking to your wife and apologizing to her for your past behavior. Tell her that you realize now what you've been doing, and that you're going to do your best to change. It may not be easy for you to rid yourself of ingrained habits, but you can do it—especially if she helps you by refusing to allow you to treat her as a maid any longer.

If she wants to wait on you once in a while, fine—just as long as she allows you to wait on her once in a while too. After all, people who are in love ought to enjoy doing things for each other. But that has to be a two-way street, and if all the traffic is headed in the same direction, something is wrong.

Remember that earlier I advised you to do things for her. Buy her some flowers just because you love her, take her out to a fancy restaurant to celebrate "nothing special" day. Bring her little surprises that will brighten up her daily life and show her that you love her.

However, please don't be like a client of mine who told me that he followed my advice, and it didn't work.

"Why not? What happened?"

"Well, I bought her a pair of slippers to surprise her."

"And?"

"And she didn't seem to appreciate it at all. In fact, she seemed really put out with me."

"Well, I can't imagine why—"

"Me neither. And I did a great job of surprising her. I hinted around like I'd bought her some expensive jewelry!"

No wonder the poor woman was a bit upset. She thought she was getting a diamond necklace and wound up with a pair of house slippers!

So surprise your wife, sure! But make sure that all your surprises are pleasant ones.

Early in our marriage I made the colossal mistake of buying my wife a toaster for Mother's Day. One of our children still remembers Mom crying that day. Dumb me. I thought she'd be pleased (it was a four-slice model). What a great psychologist, huh? Well, I've since learned a thing or two.

3. DON'T CONFUSE A RELATIONSHIP WITH A RESCUE OPERATION

Some men, and this is especially true of Firstborns, make a mistake of always "rescuing" damsels in distress.

As soon as they see a woman who needs help, their hearts start to melt and they believe they're in love. There are three reasons for this and any or all of them may come into play:

A. Genuine compassion is mistaken for love.

B. There is a need to be needed.

C. There is a chauvinistic attitude that a woman should be totally dependent upon her man. Thus, whenever he sees a woman who is likely to be dependent upon him, it reinforces his worth as a man.

Women often make the mistake of looking for a "knight in shining armor" to come along and rescue them from whatever troubles they have. That's one of the reasons the movie *An Officer and a Gentleman* was so popular a few years ago. In the final scene of the movie, pretty Debra Winger is slaving away in a factory. Suddenly Richard Gere, resplendent in his white naval uniform appears, walks into the factory, sweeps her into his arms, and carries her from the premises. Where are they headed? Obviously, they're off to the land of happily ever after.

That movie was a tremendous success at the box office, and it gained wide praise as a "woman's movie."

A fantasy like that isn't going to hurt anyone as long as we accept it for what it is—a fantasy—and realize that real life is not likely to parallel a fairy tale.

But while a woman may be making the mistake of looking for a knight, or even overlooking her boyfriend's faults because she wants to believe he's a knight, it's an even bigger mistake for the man to believe he's a knight. If he has that illusion, he's only going to get himself in trouble and probably hurt somebody else.

I know of many men who have suffered from what I call the "White Knight Syndrome," but one in particular comes to mind.

Richard finally came to his senses after three or four unhappy romantic relationships in a row. His pattern was that he would fall all over the woman while she was experiencing problems in her life. But as soon as the temporary trouble had passed, he would realize that he wasn't really in love. He would try to keep the relationship going for a while, because he really didn't want to hurt anyone. But sooner or later the charade would begin to be too much for him and he'd find himself becoming sullen, angry, and argumentative.

For instance, he began dating Yvonne when he discovered that she was facing surgery for breast cancer. He had known her for a year or so but they had never gone out. As soon as he found out what she was facing, he began showering her with concern. He couldn't do enough for her or spend enough time with her. It wasn't long before he had told her that he loved her and she, in turn, was convinced that she was in love with him.

He stood by her throughout the surgery and subsequent radiation treatments. He rejoiced with her when doctors told her that the cancer had not spread, and that because of the nature of the tumor they thought there was little likelihood that it would return.

As the next few months began to go by uneventfully, Richard realized, as he had so many times before, that what he had thought was love was actually compassionate concern. It was good that he had been with Yvonne during her time of anguish, holding her hand and praying with her. But he didn't have to cross the line and allow his involvement with her to become romantic. In fact, he hadn't wanted it to happen, because he'd done so many similar things in the past, but he couldn't seem to help himself.

Now he began his usual routine of being mean and nasty, hoping that she would break off the relationship. Unfortunately for him the worse he behaved, the more understanding and patient Yvonne was. It wasn't easy, but he finally had to tell her that he didn't really love her. For two weeks after that every time he saw her—which was often because they worked together—Yvonne's eyes were red and swollen from crying. He hated himself for what he had done to her, but he couldn't go back and tell her that he did love her when he knew he didn't.

Richard had to learn to control his tendencies to be a rescuer, and to realize that he could offer a helping hand without a promise of lifelong affection.

There are many other men who need to learn the same lesson—

and hopefully they will learn it before needlessly hurting the one they meant to help.

The Firstborn Within a Marriage

What happens when your detective work leads you to a serious relationship—perhaps even into a marriage?

That's a great situation, because not too many people go into a marriage with their eyes wide open!

Now, before we move on to the other birth orders, let's take a brief look at how the Firstborn can be expected to act in the various "departments" of a marriage or relationship.

1. AT WORK

The Firstborn is probably going to spend more time on the job than his mate would like. If he's a controller, he's going to spend a great deal of his time and energy climbing that old corporate ladder, or at least trying to. If he's the compliant, pleaser type, he's also likely to spend a great deal of his time in job-related matters in an effort to please his boss and co-workers. As a matter of fact he's likely to be doing quite a bit of work that ought to be done by his co-workers, simply because he wants their approval.

For the controller his extra time spent on the job is usually going to pay off very well, and he will be able to obtain the trappings of power that he wants. The pleaser, on the other hand, is probably going to spend a great deal of his time spinning his wheels—especially if he has developed the traits of the discouraged perfectionist, who has trouble starting any project because he knows he's not going to do it perfectly. For him, if it's not perfect, it's no good at all—so why bother to start? About the discouraged perfectionist Firstborn you might say, "Never has so much been done and so little accomplished."

2 . DURING HIS LEISURE TIME

The Firstborn is usually competitive by nature, and this will show itself in the way he spends his free time. He is not the type to lie in the grass, staring up at the clouds and letting his mind wander wherever it wants to go. A Firstborn is more likely to be at the health club playing racquet ball—and you can be sure that he's playing to win.

When I say that a Firstborn is competitive by nature, that doesn't mean that he'll spend his leisure time involved in some type of competition. But he is still likely to use his leisure in a competitive sense, such as reading a book that will help him on the job, or trying to learn some new skill. It could be that he's worked long hours at the office all week, but first thing Saturday morning he's going to be out in the yard pulling weeds or tending to his shrubs. If you marry a Firstborn, one of your biggest challenges may be to get him to take it easy every once in a while!

3 . DEALING WITH FINANCES

How often do you balance your checkbook? If you're a Firstborn you probably balance it once a month, and most likely on the day your bank statement arrives in the mail. What do you do if you try to balance your checkbook and you're off by ninety-three cents?

If you're a Last Born you probably say, "Hey, that was close enough," and forget about it. Personally, as a Last Born, I just let the bank worry about it. I've found that they really are quite good about calling when they need some *dinero.* A Firstborn, though, would probably spend a couple of hours trying to find his error, and then lose sleep over it if he couldn't find it.

Firstborns in general are very careful when it comes to money. They aren't necessarily tight, or stingy, but neither are they the type of people to go around spending money unnecessarily or foolishly. When a Firstborn buys a new car, for instance, you can bet he's researched all the back issues of *Consumer Reports* relating to new cars and knows exactly what he's doing.

Firstborns, as we've already seen, are nothing if not organized, and this is true of their financial matters as in most areas of life. The Firstborn has a natural inclination to plan for the future, to invest his money, and so forth. I'm not saying that all Firstborns are financial geniuses. But it is true that Firstborns in general give a fair amount of thought to keeping their finances in shape.

If you're married to a Firstborn it might make you angry once in a while that he can't be more impulsive in his spending. But you're probably going to be quite happy about his handling of financial matters in the long run.

4. IN HIS SOCIAL RELATIONSHIPS

The Firstborn is probably not going to be the life of the party, but that's okay because he doesn't want to be.

He may have a terrific sense of humor or he may be a great storyteller—but he's more at home displaying his talents in front of a few close friends than he would be carrying on in front of a roomful of people.

The Firstborn is quite content with a few close friends, thank you. He's not an unfriendly person and may have a great many acquaintances, but if you ask him who his really good friends are, he can probably count them off on the fingers of one hand.

If you're married to a Firstborn and you've been invited to a huge party, you may have to drag him all the way there, leaving skidmarks from his shoes every inch of the way. But if you're talking about a more intimate gathering with two or three other couples, that's no problem.

When I say you'll have to drag him to the big party I am, of course, kidding. Many Firstborns are perfectly at ease within that type of setting and may even take on the role of "life of the party." But way down deep, if the Firstborn had his druthers, he'd probably be home, curled up with a good book or his computer.

5. IN THE BEDROOM

A Firstborn can be a terrific lover—caring, giving, and passionate.

If there is any problem area in the Firstborn's sexual life, it may be that he is a bit too organized. Remember that he doesn't like surprises, so don't expect that it's going to be easy to seduce your Firstborn wife or husband in the backseat of the car at the drive-in. You may be able to talk him or her into leaving the drive-in early and heading for home, but making love is usually reserved for the bedroom, with the shades drawn, the lights out, and after the kids are all safely in bed!

Let me add right here that since I myself am married to a Firstborn, it would be well worth leaving that movie early—even if you never do find out "whodunit."

Where Firstborn males are concerned, if the man has been spoiled by his parents—particularly his mother—and always been given the best of everything, he is likely to look at sex as an area where he gets rather than gives. In other words, he may lose patience with his wife, he won't enjoy sexual foreplay, and he's merely interested in sex because it makes him feel good.

However, even though these may be his natural inclinations, he can change his ways if he really loves his sexual partner. He needs to know, though, what his wife wants and expects from him, and it may take patience on her part before he gets to the point where he's responding to her sexually the way she wants him to.

On the other extreme, the driven, overachieving Firstborn may tend to see sex as a competition. If he does, he'll be trying so hard to perform that sex becomes a chore for him rather than a pleasure.

6. IN PARENTING

One particular problem in parenting is that each birth order over-identifies with the child who is in the same birth order as he was. For example, the parent who is a Firstborn will overidentify with the Firstborn child. This usually means that the Firstborn parent, for instance, will show favoritism to the Firstborn child. But it may also mean that the Firstborn parent will be tougher on the Firstborn child. That's because he sees himself reflected in his child's attitudes and behavior, and it's not easy to see someone making the same stupid mistakes we made when we were kids.

It is true, you know, that the faults we have ourselves are the faults we can least tolerate in others.

The Firstborn as a parent is usually a tough disciplinarian and that's good, as long as he doesn't overdo it.

If the Firstborn was brought up in a home where he was always expected to do the best, be the best, and achieve, achieve, achieve, he is probably going to treat his children the same way. That can be good, again, if he doesn't overdo it and if he is happy with his children when they've tried hard, whatever the results of those efforts might have been. But it can be very bad if he is the type of parent who will never let one of his children settle for a second- or third-place finish.

This sort of parent, who is almost always a Firstborn, is continuing a cycle of defeat and frustration and is rearing children who will never live up to their potential because they're afraid of failure. Firstborn parents very often are flaw pickers, conveying clearly that the Firstborn child simply doesn't measure up to their expectations.

If you are married to a Firstborn, when it comes to raising children, you are more than likely going to have to be a moderating force insofar as discipline is concerned. You will also have to urge your mate to be more patient with the kids and get him to see that kids are little people who are ultimately going to have to make their own decisions in life.

Who knows? If you work on him hard enough, that Firstborn husband of yours just might wind up lying out on the grass with the kids, all of them looking up at the clouds drifting by and letting their minds wander wherever they want to go!

7. WHEN IT COMES TO STRESS

What do we know about the Firstborn?

We've said that he's punctual, organized, stubborn, moody, that he doesn't like surprises, etcetera.

Does this sound like someone who might get stressed out?
You bet it does.

The Firstborn may take things too seriously and he won't take his responsibilities lightly.

I am including stress in this list because we're understanding more and more what a negative force stress can be in someone's life. Pent-up stress can and does kill, and Firstborns as a class are far more stressed out than the other birth orders.

Furthermore, if you don't believe that stress is one of the "departments" of marriage, then you have either never been married or else I'd like to know your secret!

Stress can be managed, and it's important that the hard-driving Firstborn learns how to do it. If he doesn't, he'd better keep his insurance paid up and his prayers said, because he could be heading for a heart attack or stroke.

It's not my purpose here to tell you how to deal with stress. There are dozens of excellent books on the subject. But I am merely going to say that stress can be a major problem for the Firstborn, and his marriage partner would be doing him a tremendous favor by helping him learn how to deal with it.

8. IN RELIGION AND PHILOSOPHY

The Firstborn is conservative by nature, and this holds true in the area of religion.

If Mom and Dad were God-fearing people who never missed a church service in all their lives, then their Firstborn daughter is most likely going to follow suit. But then again, if his parents were Reformed Druids who danced naked on the streets of Chicago during January, Sonny Boy is probably going to do the same thing.

It is not the tendency of the Firstborn to question the beliefs of his parents, and this is what I mean by saying that he is "conservative." If his parents taught him that God exists and loves him very much, he probably won't have any trouble believing that himself.

If, on the other hand, the parents were skeptics who never could quite figure out what they believed in, their Firstborn offspring is probably going to live his life in the same shadowy land of uncertainty—no matter how much he may want to come to some definite conclusion about the meaning of life.

PART THREE

For Middle Borns Only

5

The Malleable Middles: Too Much Compromise?

O kay, Middle Borns, I know you've already counted the pages of the various sections of this book. You know how many the Firstborns are getting, how many the Last Borns are having directed at them, and you also know that they're both getting more than you are.

You're not really surprised, are you? After all, you have the fewest number of photos in the family album, and your mother sometimes has trouble remembering your name.

But that doesn't mean you're any less important.

Actually, advice given to Firstborns and Last Borns applies directly to Middle Children, too, since the Middle Child is going to be a variation on either one of those themes.

Before I get started talking about Middle Borns, dating, and marriage, let me confess right up front that this is going to be the hardest section of the book to write.

Why? Because telling you what Middle Borns are going to be like when it comes to marriage is a little bit like trying to nail gelatin to a board. There are simply so many variations of Middle-

Born personalities that it is difficult to make hard-and-fast statements about this birth order.

Some Middle Borns are very much like Firstborns, whereas others go off in the direction of the baby. It is true, then, that a marriage between two Middle Borns can on occasion work out splendidly, just as long as they are Middle Borns who will complement each other's personality.

However, if there is one particular problem that I've seen again and again within a romantic relationship involving two Middle Borns, it's a tendency to compromise the life out of their relationship. There is nothing in the least bit wrong or unhealthy about being willing to subjugate your feelings for the benefit of someone you love. But the problem with two Middle Borns is that they may wind up settling for a life-style that neither one of them wants, simply because neither one is able to express his desires in a clear and strong way.

For instance, it's Saturday night at the Joneses, and they're planning on a big night on the town. Mr. and Mrs. Jones, who are both Middle Borns, don't know yet where they're going to go, but they have the sitter lined up, some money to spend, and they're looking forward to an evening of fun and excitement.

Through the magic of our hidden microphone let's listen in on a conversation between them. Our amazing microphone is also able to tell us what people are really thinking no matter what they say, and that information is printed in parentheses:

MR. JONES: "Honey, what do you feel like doing tonight? You want to take in a movie or go dancing?" *(I hope you don't want to go dancing. I always think people are watching me, and I feel so clumsy.)*

MRS. JONES: "Anything's fine with me. You decide." *(I'd love to go dancing, but of course, you wouldn't want to do that.)*

MR. JONES: "It really doesn't matter to me either. You'd probably rather go dancing, though, wouldn't you?" *(Oh, please say dinner and a movie is fine with you!)*

MRS. JONES: "No, really. What we do doesn't matter one way or the other to me. I just want to have a good time." *(Of course I'd rather go dancing, but I'm not going to tell you that and then see you grit your teeth all evening. But if you take me to another Clint Eastwood movie, I'm going to scream!)*

MR. JONES: "Well, I really don't mind dancing if that's what you want to do." *(I can't believe I'm saying this. Won't I ever learn when to keep my mouth shut?)*

MRS. JONES: "Honey, I honestly don't care." *(What am I saying? He's offered several times to take me dancing and I know that's what I really want to do. Why can't I admit it?)*

MR. JONES: "Well, the new Meryl Streep movie is playing at the Cineplex." *(Boy! That new Clint Eastwood movie looks terrific!)*

MRS. JONES: "Sounds great to me!" *(Well, I blew it. I'll probably never get another chance to go dancing. But at least I won't have to sit through another violent Clint Eastwood film.)*

By now I'm sure you get the picture of what life is like for a couple of Middle Borns, whether they're married to each other or simply involved in a dating relationship. Those who are Middle Borns are masters of negotiation and compromise. The problem, though, is that they are often so good at negotiation because they are afraid to tell you how they really feel. They don't want to do anything that would tend to rock the boat. All they want is smooth sailing, and whenever they see the least bit of stormy weather on the horizon they'll run away from it.

The problem for Mr. and Mrs. Jones here is that neither has admitted to the other what he really wants to do. The result is that they're compromising, but in the process they're winding up doing something neither really wants to do, and so neither one is really happy. (No offense meant to Meryl Streep.) And you can bet that if they aren't able to admit their true feelings to each other regarding whether to go dancing or to see the latest Clint Eastwood flick, they're hiding their feelings from each other in a number of other areas too.

Put two Middle Borns together and you're not going to get an explosive combination as you will with two First Borns. As a matter of fact, this is not that bad a combination. But problems do arise when two people who have spent their lives together compromising and playing down their own feelings suddenly realize that they're tired of never getting to do what they really want to do.

True, this is a natural trait that the Middle Born learned early in his life, but he doesn't like it, and it causes resentment to build toward his partner—even though it's not the partner's fault.

Suppose Susan and her husband and their kids have taken a vacation trip to the mountains every year for the last five years. They've slept in tents, cooked fish over an open fire, and generally behaved like a group of pioneers.

Susan has always hated camping, and she's not too fond of a steady diet of rainbow trout. But she's always smiled and pretended that it was the most fun thing in the world, simply because she knew her husband, Ralph, loved it.

Ralph, on the other hand, who is also a Middle Born, likes camping, sure enough, and he loves to fish, but he's kind of tired of doing the same thing every year. In fact, he'd love to take the kids to Disney World or maybe to the beach, just once. He never says anything about it, though, because he knows how much these trips to the mountains mean to his wife.

This year when they're planning their annual trip, all of Susan's pent-up emotions can no longer be contained and come exploding into the open. She simply cannot take one more night of sleeping in that tent, and the very thought of it sends her into a rage.

"Why do we always have to go to the mountains! I hate the mountains! I hate the bugs, the dirt, the smelly old fish, and I hate you too!" She doesn't mean that last part, but it's too late to take it back once she's said it.

"What are you talking about? I thought you loved the mountains!" Ralph can't believe what he's hearing.

"That shows how much you know! You never even consider my feelings. You just assume I'll want to do anything you want to do!"

"That's not fair! I'm always sacrificing my own desires for you! What makes you think I'm so gung-ho about sleeping in a tent for two weeks?"

At this point the fight is just getting started, and believe me, it's going to be a doozy before it's through. It's started over where the family goes for its vacation, but before it's over, every resentment that has been building up for the last several years is probably going to be trotted out.

In the name of compromise and peace both Susan and Ralph have allowed these resentments and other garbage to build up in their lives, and now that the dams that have held them back have come tumbling down, look out!

This is one of the primary problems for Middle Borns. They let problems, which may be minor in the beginning, build up and grow to the point where they become overwhelming. What was once a slight resentment is now a Grand Canyon of bitterness, and there's no way to build a bridge across a canyon like that!

Have you ever had dandelions in your yard? Chances are you have, because those ornery little suckers are everywhere, and if you give them an inch, they'll take a mile.

Whenever I see the first sign of one of those little yellow heads poking through the grass in my lawn, I'm out there digging it up before it has a chance to beckon its brothers and sisters. I know what would happen if I ignored that first little dandelion, and so do you. Within a couple of weeks my entire lawn would be covered with a blanket of yellow.

I could have dealt with that first dandelion simply and in a matter of moments. Now, because I waited so long, it's going to take me hours of backbreaking labor to get my lawn back in decent shape.

Think of my lawn—or better yet, your lawn—covered with dandelions and you get the picture of what a couple of Middle Borns would allow to happen in their relationship. They don't deal with anger and get it out of their system, and if there's anything that can spread faster than dandelions, it's anger.

Now, it may not be a decision regarding where to go for vacation that causes problems for a couple of Middle Borns. Chances are that Susan would have at least been able to suggest after the second or third year that maybe they should go somewhere else the following year. But the problems that come between a couple of Middle Borns are likely to be just as trivial. Remember, though, that a nuclear explosion starts with the splitting of a single atom!

Looking back over what's happened between Susan and Ralph, is it really Ralph's fault that the family has gone camping all these years when Susan really didn't want to go? Truthfully Susan should be just at angry at herself as she is with her husband. If she had told him five years ago that camping wasn't her favorite all-time thing to do, and if she hadn't pretended to have had such a good time on their first camping trip, she wouldn't have spent the last five summers swatting mosquitoes and trying to get the fishy smell off her hands.

On the other hand it's not entirely Susan's fault either. For one thing, Ralph certainly should have been more open with her about his own feelings, as in "Honey, I know you really love camping, but I think it would be nice if we could do something different this year." For another thing, he should have been more perceptive and able to discern his wife's true feelings. Surely during those years, she would have given him many signals that her "love" of camping was just a front, and he should have been able to pick up on those signals.

Any man in general needs to learn to read his ladylove's mind, and this is especially true if his ladylove is a Middle Born.

Now, I can hear some man saying, "What are you talking about? Why should I learn to read her mind? Let her learn to read mine instead."

Well, you see, the truth is that she probably does a pretty good job of reading your mind. As a general rule women are much more perceptive when it comes to interpersonal relationships. They are more able to "read between the lines" and better at picking up on the subtle clues of body language and gestures.

Men are more apt to take things at face value. We don't always see the subtle innuendos behind what people are saying, and we are not so interested in getting beneath the surface to find out what other people are really all about.

Women, in general, are more relationship-oriented and more concerned about what people are really thinking.

So here's a marriage between two Middle Borns. Now, suppose the husband comes home from work on a Friday night and discovers that the kids have all gone off to spend the night with friends. Perhaps his wife just got home from work, too, and she's looking in the refrigerator to see what she wants to fix for dinner.

Hubby has a good idea, though, and he says those three little words that every woman wants to hear: "Out to dinner."

She looks at him as if he really is the white knight she thought he was before she found out that he snores and leaves little hairs in the sink.

By the time the husband gets to the car, he finds his wife has been waiting there for a couple of minutes. That's because he walked to the car, but she flew.

"So . . . where do you want to go tonight?"

You know what the answer's going to be, don't you?

"Oh, I really don't care. Anything is fine with me."

Now, you see, the visions that are running through her head have to do with cozy little French restaurants and steak places. Certainly nowhere that doesn't have an extensive wine list.

But her husband isn't operating on quite that wavelength. When he talks about going out for dinner, he's thinking of someplace where he can get something to eat, period. Atmosphere, or lack thereof, doesn't even come to mind.

"You sure you don't have any place in mind?" he says.

"No. You decide."

Hubby, who has never learned to read her mind, thinks, *Well, if*

*she doesn't care, and the kids aren't around, maybe we should just
go get a quick bite to eat.*

"Honey, what do you say we run down to Mickey D's Golden
Arches?"

She looks at him and says, "McDonald's?" From the fire in her
eyes you would think he had asked her to dine on nuts and wild
berries instead of hamburgers and fries. Hopefully he's smart
enough now to know that she doesn't care where they go, just so
long as it's someplace that employs a maître d'. But if he's still so
unaware of her true feelings that he does take her to see Mickey D,
all the neighbors had better stay in their houses tonight, because
there's going to be a fireworks display!

I discuss that scenario from time to time at seminars and I can
always tell by the laughter that most married couples have been
through a similar incident. And I'm never surprised to discover
that the ones who laugh loudest and longest are the Middle
Borns.

How Well Do You Communicate
with Your Mate?

Redbook magazine once published a quiz that was designed to
uncover obstacles to communication that may exist between a husband and wife. I thought the quiz was excellent, and to help you
see what problems there might be in your marriage—or in your
current relationship—and discover ways you might overcome
them, I am reprinting an abridged and modified version of that
quiz here.[1]

First, for women only:

1. Your birthday is coming up. The man in your life very often
   forgets, so you:
   A. wait to see whether he remembers
   B. drop hints
   C. remind him

2. If you have a problem with your husband or boyfriend, with whom will you first discuss it?
   A. No one
   B. A friend or close relative
   C. Him
3. Your guy really hurt your feelings. Do you:
   A. tell him so?
   B. give him the cold shoulder for a while?
   C. lash out and hurt him back?
4. If something terribly embarrassing happened to you, would you tell him about it?
   A. No
   B. Maybe
   C. Probably
5. Baseball bores you to death, but your man could discuss it for hours. When the subject comes up, you:
   A. explain how bored you are and ask him to talk about something else
   B. change the subject yourself as soon as possible
   C. work on showing some interest
6. You had an unsuccessful job interview at lunchtime and you're very upset. Your husband comes home from work looking downcast and you:
   A. wait until he's in a better mood to tell him all about it
   B. tell him you didn't get the job but try to hide your emotional reaction
   C. begin pouring out your story the moment he takes off his coat
7. For the second time this month your husband has left practically no gas in the car. Do you:
   A. leave the tank empty and see how he likes it?
   B. leave it empty but let him know in advance so he can allow himself time for a gas station stop?
   C. fill up the tank but tell him you're annoyed?

And now, for men only:

1. When your lady is in a bad mood, you are likely to:
    A. ask whether she's getting her period
    B. leave her alone until she's feeling better
    C. ask her what's wrong
2. She says you don't tell her often enough that you love her. You reply:
    A. "That's your problem, not mine."
    B. "You know I love you. Why do I have to say it?"
    C. "I love you very much. Sometimes I just forget to say so."
3. At dinner with the kids your wife mentions that she'd like to talk to you later, alone. You say:
    A. "How about ten o'clock?"
    B. "Okay, anytime you want."
    C. "Sorry, I'm going bowling."
4. How often do you win arguments with your wife or girlfriend?
    A. Almost always
    B. Almost never
    C. I try not to think in terms of winning or losing
5. Your lady wants to talk about some difficulties she's having at work. Would you most likely:
    A. point out that you have work problems of your own?
    B. offer advice?
    C. listen and try to be supportive?
6. For the second time this month you find that your wife has left the car's gas tank empty. Annoyed, you:
    A. fill it, then tell her how much this irritates you
    B. leave it empty but let her know so she can plan on stopping at a gas station
    C. leave it empty to see how she likes it
7. You're in the mood to make love, but when you reach for her she just yawns. You:

    A. roll over and go to sleep, feeling rejected

    B. ask her why she isn't responding

    C. cuddle up and just hold her until you both fall asleep

To see how you fare in the quiz, for questions one, two, four, five, and seven give yourself one point for each A answer, two for each B, and three for each C. Then on questions three and six give yourself three points for each A, two for each B, and one for every C.

First, the ladies:

7–11 points: You're going to have to put more effort into the communication process if you want to be more satisfied in the relationship. You need to try to express yourself without becoming defensive—making more statements about how you feel and fewer accusations about your partner's behavior. Blaming him for your problems is certain to block all communication between you.

12–17 points: You're not doing badly, but there are some sensitive spots in your makeup that tend to block communication. You not only have to hear what your partner is saying, but also offer feedback to make sure you are hearing him properly.

18–21 points: You and your lover probably do a very good job of communicating with each other. But remember—there's always room for improvement.

Now for the men:

7–11 points: Remember that to hide your feelings from the woman in your life is one of the fastest ways you can ruin a relationship. Learn how to listen to her and learn how to talk to her— before your marriage goes up in an explosion of silence!

12–17 points: You're doing well, but you need to remember that your lady needs your support and encouragement much more than she needs your "practical advice." Give more effort to trying to see things from your wife's point of view, and you'll see your relationship improve.

18–21 points: You're doing quite well in the area of communication with your lover, but, as I said before, there is always room for improvement.

Trouble in the Bedroom

Sex is another particularly troubling area for two Middle Borns who wind up married to each other. They are not as likely to tell each other their likes and dislikes when it comes to the conjugal bed. Nor are they likely to be honest with each other regarding the desire for intimacy.

For instance, here's Joe and Jodi, two Middle Borns, lying in bed on a Friday night. They've just turned out the lights, and the house is quiet.

Joe reaches over and pats his wife's hand. "Good night, sweet-heart."

Jodi squeezes his hand and snuggles in close beside him. He thinks, *Is she just trying to get comfortable, is she trying to tell me she loves me, or does she have something else on her mind?*

He pats her hand again. "How you feeling tonight, hon?"

"Fine," comes the answer. "And how are you?"

"I'm fine too."

There's a minute of silence now, as both of them wait to see if the other one is going to say anything else.

Joe clears his throat. "Well, I was just wondering . . . you know . . . if you're sleepy, or maybe, you know. . . ." It's funny, because they've been married for ten years, and he still can't bring himself to flat-out tell his wife that he would really like to make love to her tonight.

Jodi says, "No. I'm not really sleepy. I'm okay, though. How do you feel?"

Her husband responds, "Well, I wouldn't mind, you know . . . fooling around or something . . . if it sounds okay to you."

Well, they started the conversation at eleven P.M., but by the time they decide whether or not they're going to make love, it's probably well past midnight. They may even fall asleep in the middle of talking about it and never actually get around to doing it.

I'm exaggerating, of course, but it is important for married couples to communicate with each other about sex.

It's important for wives to let their husbands know when they're "in the mood," when they're too tired, et cetera, and the same goes for husbands.

Occasionally couples who can talk to each other about everything else in the world have a great deal of trouble discussing the sexual aspect of their relationship.

I have suggested to such couples that they learn to do such things as writing little notes to each other.

The wife might put a note behind her husband's plate at dinner, *I'm feeling romantic tonight. Meet me in our bedroom at ten-thirty.* Or the husband might slip a note to his wife saying something like *You look so beautiful tonight, you take my breath away. How about getting together with me later on?* I don't care how much trouble you have verbalizing your desire for your mate, you can always write it down on a piece of paper.

Of course, the husband who expects his wife to want to meet him in the bedroom later on had better be attentive to her needs throughout the rest of the evening. He can't expect to treat her coldly all evening and then have her turn into Paulina Passionate as soon as the lights are out.

The reverse is true, too, and the woman who criticizes her husband all evening can't expect him to be wanting to kiss and hold her as soon as they're in bed together.

But I am not so concerned here with improving the sex life of Middle-Born married couples as I am with teaching them that they must learn to communicate with each other on an honest and open level. Hiding your true feelings from your spouse is not being unselfish and giving, because if he loves you he wants more than anything else for you to be truly happy. Denying him the chance to make you happy by refusing to tell him what you really want is really one of the most selfish things you can do.

Communication Is the Key

If you are a Middle Born who is married to another Middle Born, it is likely that the two of you need to improve your communication, in the bedroom as well as in every other area of your relationship. You can do that by following these four simple procedures:

1. TALK TO EACH OTHER

Commit yourselves to talking to each other for thirty minutes every night before you go to bed.

What are you supposed to talk about? That is entirely up to you. The important thing is that you are communicating with each other. You can bring up problems if you want to, or just tell each other about the day you've had.

Be able to tell each other even the most trivial things that happened to you during the day, and be willing and ready to listen to your partner talk about the day he or she has had. In talking to each other about those little experiences that happen every day you'll really get to know each other better, and you'll sharpen your communication skills.

Does your ladylove know what you're doing all day at work? Does she know what you think of the people you work with—the petty annoyances that come your way or the little events that lift your spirits during the day?

Does the man in your life know what you're doing during the day when he's not around?

Tell each other about it. Love means that finding out about those little things is important.

When it comes to the art of conversation, I will always believe that the best thing you can do is to talk about the other person— show some interest in him and he'll think you're a scintillating conversationalist. It also helps to show some interest in the things he's interested in.

For instance, is he crazy about football? Why not take a look at the sports page and find out a thing or two about what's going on in the sport. He'll be pleasantly surprised that you took the time to learn about something that interests him so much.

Is she excited about a particular local issue that hasn't interested you? Well, read up on it and get interested in it. Show her that her interests are important to you, and your relationship will be enhanced.

2. SAY SOMETHING ABOUT YOUR RELATIONSHIP

There is one stipulation, and that is that each of you must try to make at least one statement—good or bad—about your relationship.

For instance, "Honey, when we were sitting at the table after dinner tonight and you reached over and patted my hand, that meant a lot to me. Sometimes it's those little things you do that let me know you love me, and I just wanted you to know I appreciate it."

Or "You know, you left for work this morning without giving me a hug and a kiss good-bye. That made me feel kind of bad, because it's important to me. It starts the day off right, letting me know that you love me."

Perhaps you'll just want to reaffirm your love for each other, as in "I love you, hon, and I'm awfully glad I got you." It doesn't have to be a long, detailed discussion of the relationship, but it does have to be something that expresses how you feel about where you are in the relationship.

3. IF YOU CAN'T SAY IT, WRITE IT OUT

You may have trouble talking openly about your relationship at first, so you may want to supplement these little talks with written communication.

Both of you should agree to keep the lines of communication flowing, and that means putting down in writing what you find yourself unable to say in person. Now, these notes aren't supposed to be hard-hitting accusations. There isn't any need to get nasty. If there is a problem, it should be stated as clearly, but as gently, and in as nonthreatening a way, as possible.

4. DON'T OVERDO IT

Now, it's true that some Middle Borns go wildly from one side of the spectrum to the other. At first they have trouble expressing their true feelings at all. But then, later on, once they find out that it's okay to have opinions, they start having opinions about everything. Strong opinions! In some cases abrasive opinions! What they're doing, you see, is making up for lost time—all those years when they were afraid to tell anyone how they really felt because they didn't want a confrontation. When this happens, you have to rein them in and say, "Please, express yourself. But do it gently!"

All Types of Middle Borns

I mentioned earlier that it's hard to typecast a relationship between two Middle Borns. Part of the reason for this is that there are almost as many types of Middle Borns as there are stars in the sky.

That's because there are families of all different shapes and sizes. For instance, suppose there is a family of eight children. It's possible, although not really probable, that those born into the second through seventh positions would all be Middle Borns. At the same time all of them would have widely different influences operating on them. The second-born child would feel tremendous impact from the personality of the oldest child, while the third-born would be shaped in equal measure by the personalities of the first two, and so on.

And then there are Middle-Born boys who come from families in which all the children were boys, Middle-Born females whose siblings were all girls, as well as Middle Borns who had siblings of the opposite sex.

Some studies have found that marriages are more likely to succeed if each of the partners had siblings of the opposite sex, and this is true in marriages involving two Middle Borns. In this situation each of the partners has grown up feeling comfortable around members of the opposite sex. He and she have come to understand that gender differences go deeper than the anatomy, and both are apt to have a better understanding of the attitudes and psychological needs of the opposite sex.

If you want to gain a better understanding of your Middle-Born spouse, you need to take a long, hard look at his or her siblings, and especially the older ones. Keep in mind, though, that a second-born female with an older brother may actually develop the characteristics of a Firstborn instead of a Middle Born, although she is most likely to have some of the characteristics of both. And, of course, the same is true of a boy who was the second child born into his family, but who has an older sister.

Remember what we said earlier, that in order to avoid conflict and direct competition a Middle Child will very often go off in a sharply opposite direction from the Firstborn child. For instance, if the Firstborn is a scholastic ace who never met a course he couldn't conquer, the Middle Born is likely to let schoolwork slide and excel in sports, music, or clownmanship. If he feels he can't compete with his older sibling on an equal footing, he'll find his own route to "success," even if he is only interested in being the best at being the worst. (At least that means he'll be good at something.)

All of these factors enter, then, into the makeup of the Middle-Born child and explain why one marriage between two Middle Borns may be so different from another.

Let's take a brief look at a few of the various types of marriages featuring Middle Borns:

Female Second Born with male Second Born: The strength and shape of this marriage depends to a great degree on whether the Second Borns in this case have taken on many of the characteristics of the Firstborn. You could wind up here with a couple of

VARIOUS MIDDLE-BORN
RELATIONSHIPS AND
THEIR TRAITS

FEMALE SECOND BORN   **MALE SECOND BORN**

   +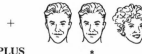

*   PLUS   *

Both could be strong-willed, competitive people, or deferential types who step aside to let the other take charge.

FEMALE SECOND BORN   **MALE LATER-BORN MIDDLE**

   +

*   PLUS   *

The female may have drive and determination while her husband is comfortable staying in the shadows.

MALE SECOND BORN   **FEMALE LATER-BORN MIDDLE**
WITH OLDER SISTER(S)

   +

*   PLUS   *

The husband is likely to be more ambitious and ready to be head of the family. The woman will be comfortable with this, but not hesitant to take charge or express her opinions.

FEMALE LATER MIDDLE   **MALE LATER MIDDLE**

   +

*   PLUS   *

Neither one will probably be interested in taking charge and both will be hesitant to express their views.

strong-willed, competitive people, or you could have a couple of deferential types who always step aside to let the other take charge. Either way you're going to need two things: communication and compromise.

Female Second Born with male Later Middle: The female Second Born may have the drive and determination associated with the Firstborn position in the family. She may become exasperated with her husband, who, due to his birth-order position, is used to staying pretty much in the shadows and doesn't mind it there. On the other hand she may appreciate the fact that her husband is usually willing to let her have the last word in any discussion. I'm not saying for sure that this is the reason why, but it is true that male Middle Borns who are born later down the line in their families have a proportionately lower divorce rate than other birth orders.

Male Second Born who has older sister(s) with female Later-Born Middle: This is a rather comfortable combination. The husband is likely to be more ambitious and ready to assume the role of head of the family, whereas the woman in this case is ready and happy to have him do just that. You're not so likely to have two butting egos in this type of marriage, but neither will you have two people who are totally afraid to take charge and express opinions.

Female Later Middle and male Later Middle: Both of the partners in a marriage like this are likely to need a good dose of assertiveness training. Neither one is likely to be interested in taking charge, and both will be hesitant to express their views. The biggest problem here is establishing effective communication and deciding who is going to assume what responsibilities within the family.

I realize that we have barely scratched the surface with regard to the Middle Born's traits, and how those traits fit into a romantic relationship. But stay tuned, because coming up next we're going to take a closer look at what a Middle Born ought to be looking for when it comes to a lasting relationship, and then, just as we did with Firstborns, we'll give some solid advice for the Middle Born who wants to be a romantic detective!

Exercises for Middle Borns

1. Practice expressing your feelings honestly and succinctly.

2. Write a list at the end of every day of all the things you did that you didn't have to do and that you really didn't want to do. Make up your mind to see the list grow shorter every day.

3. Spend time getting to know yourself. Ask how you really feel about things and how much of your attitudes about life have been shaped by the expectations, likes, and dislikes of others.

4. Ask yourself how much of the compromising you do is really unnecessary.

5. Make a list of the personality characteristics you have that make you attractive to others.

6. Can you list some of the ways you tried to establish your own turf in your family as you were growing up? For example, if your older sibling(s) excelled in math and basketball, did you make an effort in science and baseball?

7. Search through the old family photo albums for some pictures of yourself without *them*. Then run out and buy some frames for the three or four photos you find.

6

The Middle Born Takes a Mate

It's never easy being in the middle.

Have you ever come across a beautiful poem that really stirred your soul? Perhaps you read it two or three times, letting all the beautiful words sink in, and then you looked to see who wrote it.

All it said was "author unknown."

Chances are the author of that poem was a Middle Child—and like most Middle Children he never got any recognition or credit, no matter what he did!

I'm being facetious, of course, but it does seem to be the lot of the Middle Child to stay in the shadows, lost in a sort of never-never land of anonymity. That's not always bad, though, because Middle Children usually don't get the pressure from their parents that is heaped upon First- and Last-Born children.

Pressure is put on the oldest child simply because he is the oldest and so is expected to set the standard for all the brothers and sisters who follow him.

Pressure is placed on the youngest because he is the last of the family, and so is expected to measure up to the achievements of his older brothers and sisters.

Pressure also comes to those who occupy both of these birth positions simply because they are more visible, since they occupy unique positions in the family zoo.

But while these two people get most of the pressure, they also get most of the attention and the credit.

What three words does the Middle Child hear most often as he grows up?

"That's nice, dear."

As in:

"Mom, I got straight A's."

"That's nice, dear."

"Dad, I got the lead in the school play."

"That's nice, George." (George Bush is a Middle Born.)

"Hey, Mom and Dad, I've just been elected President of the United States!"

"That's nice, dear."

Most Middle Children are soul mates to Rodney Dangerfield. They just don't get no respect!

And so far it seems that's the way it is when it comes to marriage. We've spent quite a bit of time talking about marriage as it relates to the Firstborn and the Last Born. But what about the Middle Child?

We've already seen that a marriage of two Middle Children is apt to run into trouble because of the compromising, negotiating nature of the Middle Child and their tendency to keep their true feelings to themselves.

While it is true that a partner in any successful marriage will be called on to do a fair amount of compromising, negotiating, and sacrificing of his own desires to make the other person happy, put two Middle Children together and they're likely to negotiate and compromise the life right out of the relationship.

So where does that leave us? If Firstborn–Last Born is the best marriage combination, and if a marriage of two Middle Borns is not the best in the world, that doesn't leave anywhere for Middle Borns to turn, does it?

Well, the truth is that statistics say that you, as a Middle Born, will actually have a better chance to have a successful marriage than either your older or younger siblings will.

I've mentioned before that one out of every two marriages in the United States ends in divorce. There have been several studies that have shown, though, that the divorce rate for marriages in which at least one of the partners is a Middle Born is much lower than for other couples. All in all, once Middle Borns are married, they tend to stay married. This is undoubtedly due to the Middle Born's ability to negotiate and compromise.

The Middle Born, you see, is the most monogamous and faithful of the birth orders.[1]

If you are looking for someone who's going to be faithful and true, you couldn't do any better than to seek out a Middle Child. (Just so long as you remember that though studies have shown this to be true in a general sense, no one could ever say that all Middle Children are going to be faithful, any more than one could say that all Firstborns or Only Children will have a tendency to wander. How a person behaves sexually has as much to do with his upbringing and the morality his parents have taught him as it does with his birth order. Still, find yourself a Middle Child who was brought up in a strongly moral atmosphere, and you've probably found yourself a candidate for sainthood!)

The Two Tribes of Middle Borns

Generally speaking, we can divide Middle Borns into two basic groups—and for purposes of our discussion here, we will refer to them as Early Middle Borns and Later Middle Borns.

You might think that an Early Middle Born would be most like a Firstborn, whereas the Later Middle Born would have many of the characteristics of the Last Born—but it isn't necessarily so. In fact, the opposite may be closer to the truth.

The Early Middle Born may be too close to the Firstborn to

take on many of his personality characteristics. He is more likely to react to his older brother or sister by choosing a life-style that is very different. But the Later Middle Born is a step farther removed from the Firstborn and is more likely to be directly influenced by the Early Middle Born.

Suppose, for instance, that the Johnson family has four children, all of them girls. The first girl is an outstanding student who rarely brings home a report card that isn't all A's. Furthermore, she is an excellent musician.

The Second Born, or the Early Middle Born child, learns quickly that she can't compete with her sister academically or musically, so she seeks attention by becoming a super athlete. She's the best soccer and softball player in the neighborhood, but she barely gets by at school.

By the time the third daughter gets into the first grade, her oldest sister is already in the sixth grade, so she's not going to feel the pressure as much as her immediately older sister did. As a result this girl may throw herself into academics in the same way the Firstborn did. In fact, it's quite possible that she'll emulate the oldest girl in a number of ways. It isn't the case that every additional child born into a family will be less like a Firstborn and more like a Last Born.

When I talk about Early Middle Borns I'm talking about Second Borns primarily, although we could also include those who may be born even later in very large families.

It's fairly easy to understand the personality characteristics that have been built into an Early Middle Born by his birth order. Basically all you have to do is take a look at the Firstborn child, then spend a few moments checking out Mom and Dad, and you'll have a pretty good idea of how and why this Middle Born is going to act the way he does.

But it's not so easy to figure out where the Later Middle Born is coming from. That's because he has so many influences pushing and pulling on him. Every one of his older brothers and sisters has impacted on him in some way, although you can generally know that the next oldest sibling is going to be the most influential.

For instance, suppose the Middle Born's chief influence is his older brother, who is so hard driving and ambitious that he makes Donald Trump seem lazy. Like an Arizona flash flood following the path of least resistance, Middle Born is going to be easygoing, relaxed, and probably rather otherworldly.

His best marital matchup will be with a Firstborn who has a bit of fire in her eyes. He will need someone to shake him up a bit, to help him see that you can't make it through life without showing some ambition once in a while.

If he should marry a fun-loving Last Born he's headed for trouble. Their marriage will be very similar to that of two Last Borns, who may laugh their way to the poorhouse.

If, on the other hand, his older brother was a pleaser, someone who could never seem to do enough to win someone else's approval, the Middle Born is likely to be aggressive and bold, the sort of person who is going to be a "taker" rather than a "giver" and someone who doesn't have to be on the dance floor to be stepping on a few toes.

If this person marries the go-get-'em Firstborn, what we're going to have on our hands is an instant replay of the movie *Clash of the Titans.*

What he needs is the fun-loving approach to life the Last Born can bring his way.

Let's take a look, now, at some of the more "typical" characteristics of Middle Borns, and see what those traits have to say about Middle Borns and marriage. We've already spent quite a bit of time talking about the fact that Middle Borns are very good when it comes to negotiating and working out compromises. But let's look now at some of their other characteristics, remembering that no person can have all of these traits. (Some of them, in fact, are diametrically opposed.) Middle Borns may:

1. let other people determine their personality
2. feel squeezed and closed in by their siblings
3. suffer from the "squeezed child" syndrome
4. feel inferior to others

5. be intensely loyal
6. be competitive

Admittedly, some of these traits I've listed might be regarded as "minuses" while others might be considered "pluses," but I prefer to regard them as neutrals, and almost all of them can work as positive additions to a romantic relationship.

Let's take them one at a time.

1. LETTING OTHER PEOPLE DETERMINE YOUR PERSONALITY

I don't want to keep playing the same old note, but it really is true that a great many Middle Borns feel anonymous. Not only do other people not know who they are and what they're all about, but they don't seem to know themselves.

The Middle Born is likely to have dozens of friends, and that's good. But on the other hand he is more likely than any other birth order to be shaped by peer pressure. He will let his friends' attitudes and personalities define who he is.

An acquaintance of mine couldn't understand it when his teenage daughter, who was a Middle Born, got heavily into punk music. She refused to wear clothes that were any color except black, she shaved the sides of her head, wrote poems about death and destruction, and generally acted as if she were just visiting this planet while on a vacation from her native Pluto. Did the girl like punk music? No. Did she think she looked good in black? No. Was she really obsessed with dying? No. But in all of these instances she was letting a group of punker friends define her personality for her. Admittedly, as a Middle Born she was especially susceptible to peer pressure. But a Middle Born who isn't sure who he is, is especially likely to let his prospective romantic partner mold his personality.

Back in the nineteen sixties a rock group called the American Breed had a huge hit record called "Bend Me, Shape Me." Some of the lyrics were "Bend me, shape me any way you want me, Long as you love me, it's all right."

That song is one of the great all-time anthems of the Middle Born who isn't sure who he is or what he wants out of life.

The Middle Born who is this way is the perfect "prey" for a hard-driving Firstborn who wouldn't hesitate for one minute telling someone else how to live his life. Now, I am not saying here that such a Middle Born should not marry a hard-charging Firstborn—but before he does, he had better get to know himself and find out who he is.

I know that one of the hardest things to do is to obtain an accurate picture of yourself, but you need to know who you are, and you can find out by:

—making a list of your strengths and weaknesses

—writing down the ten things you'd most like to do in life

—thinking about what you do that you really enjoy, and what you do that you don't enjoy at all

—making a list of your five closest friends and asking yourself what attracted you to each of them

—taking a long hard look at your family to see how you fit in: What have other family members come to expect from you? (More about that in a moment.)

—spending some time alone with your own thoughts, away from the influences of others

Most of us tend to think we're pretty good people. We see ourselves as thoughtful, kind, giving people, and we're pretty sure that most folks like us. Even most people who are bothered with low self-esteem know that deep down inside they're good people. They may feel incompetent or inadequate in some ways, but they still don't doubt their innate goodness.

It is important, though, to have a realistic view of yourself, especially if you're considering marriage. Not only do you need to know what your prospective mate will have to put up with, but it's a good idea to know what sort of partner will make you happiest.

It's hard to step back and say, "You know, I'm afraid I take life too seriously. I need to slow down and have some fun once in a while."

Meanwhile the person who lives for the thrill of the moment isn't likely to take the time to analyze his existence and realize that "I can't go on living like this. I've got to make something out of myself, before it's too late."

But if you really want to have a successful marriage—and I'd go so far as to say if you want a successful life—you really do need to take stock of yourself.

If you're a Middle Child, take some time to think about the forces that have shaped and molded you into the person you are today, and that means, primarily, your family.

Take a long hard look at your parents, looking longest and hardest at your opposite-sex parent. Ask yourself questions like these:

—What sort of attitude did my parents try to instill in me?

—Did my father (or mother) encourage and support me, or was he the sort who found fault with everything I did?

—What character trait of my father's (or mother's) would I most like to have in my own life?

—What character trait would I most want to avoid having in my life?

—What are the most important things I learned from my parents?

—When am I most like my father (or mother)?

—When am I least like my father (or mother)?

Once you've taken stock of your parents, do the same thing with your older brothers and sisters. Not only are you likely to discover things about them you never knew, but you will also learn a great many things about yourself in the process.

Let me say it again—the key to understanding your partner, and thus to having a successful marriage, is first to understand yourself.

I remember one woman who made a startling discovery about herself just by watching her five-year-old daughter play with her dolls.

One day Mom was going into her daughter's room to put up some clothes she had just taken out of the dryer. The girl had one of her dolls in its high chair while she pretended to feed it.

"I told you to eat your breakfast and you'd better do it right now," she said. She had such a serious, threatening edge to her voice that Mom just had to laugh.

But she stopped laughing when the little girl kept berating her doll: "You're just a naughty girl! You better watch out or you're going to get it! Do you want a spanking?"

Over the next few days Mom watched closely every time the little girl was playing with her doll, and always saw the same thing: Little Nicole was always shaking her finger in the doll's face, telling her what a bad girl she was and threatening physical punishment.

How did Nicole get those attitudes? There was only one way she could have picked them up, and that was from her mother.

Painful tears stung Mom's eyes as she realized that she was treating her little girl in pretty much the same way the girl was treating her doll. She'd never realized it before, but the truth was that she was passing on the supercritical fault-finding attitude she had picked up from her own parents. Right now Nicole was only berating her doll, but Mom was smart enough to realize that if she didn't do something to change things, it wouldn't be too many years before Nicole would be dishing out the same sort of treatment to her own daughter.

Mom realized, too, that she was treating her husband almost as badly as she was treating her daughter. It was horrible to see herself the way she really was, and she locked herself in her bedroom and cried for nearly an hour. But she also resolved to change, to learn to hold her tongue, and to think before saying anything in anger.

Now, in defense of Mom, I have to say that she was merely

continuing the pattern that had been established by her own parents.

This woman not only had to forgive herself for the way she had acted toward her daughter, and resolve not to continue treating the girl that way—but she also had to look at her relationship with her own mother and resolve to bring forgiveness into that relationship.

As I've sat behind closed doors for twenty years, sorting through hundreds if not thousands of people's lives, I've been impressed with the fact that so many of us grew up in environments that were anything but sane. So maybe lots of things have happened to you and there have been many psychological bumps and bruises. When you realize that, the tendency these days is to get angry and vent that anger on your parents, who with very little training or expertise tried to accomplish the complex job of parenthood the best they could. The key to happiness and security is never found in pummeling good ol' Ma and Pa, however, but in forgiving them and moving on with life.

Take a close look at your parents, and chances are you will be taking a look in a mirror—however unclear or distorted the reflection may be. This doesn't mean that you are destined to follow in your parents' footsteps and that there's nothing you can do about it. But you may unwittingly be making some of the same mistakes your parents made, and the first step toward making a successful change in your behavior is to recognize that a change needs to be made.

Another friend of mine told me about the shocking self-realization he'd gotten when he took his children to a water theme park one hot July afternoon. Sometime during the middle of the day he took the kids to a concession stand to buy some ice cream. That's when, in his words, "I happened to catch a glimpse of some fat guy in a bathing suit.

"My first thought was *Boy, that guy needs to lose some weight,* and then a horrible thought hit me. I backed up a few paces and, yep, sure enough, what I had seen was my own reflection in the window of the gift shop."

Not a pleasant experience, to be sure. And yet my friend turned this painful occurrence into something positive. After doing his best to keep his stomach sucked in for the rest of the day, he went home determined to be more sensible in his diet and to start a regular exercise program—both of which he needed.

Middle Born, what kind of person are you? No one can answer that question the way you can answer it for yourself. But you must resolve to take a long, honest look. You might see a critical woman who isn't very nice to be around, but if that's what you see, be thankful that you've learned something about yourself and that you can work to change things. You might see a fat guy in a bathing suit, but even then, you can do something about it.

2. FEELING SQUEEZED AND CLOSED IN BY YOUR SIBLINGS

It's easy to understand why the Middle Born would feel squeezed and closed in. He's always surrounded, at home, at school, wherever he goes. To some extent he's always being compared to his siblings, and he's never allowed to be "just himself."

What happens when the Middle Born who spends his early years feeling squeezed becomes an adult? He feels he's never been allowed to be an individual. He's always been just another cog in the machinery of the family, always rather anonymous, never getting the attention of the youngest or oldest, never really being allowed to shine. Well, you can bet that as an adult he's going to rebel against the role he's always held. He's likely to be the free spirit who disregards tradition and who seeks to do everything in a different way. This can be very good if he seeks to express his rebellious nature in good ways. He can be creative and spontaneous, and that certainly isn't bad.

But it can be a problem if he marries someone who acts the same way, whether that person is another Middle Born or a Last Born.

The free-spirited Middle Born may have a hard time accepting it, but his ideal partner is someone who is going to keep him reined in a bit. This usually translates out to a Firstborn who knows that some rules and regulations are necessary—or who at least knows that there will be painful consequences to follow if those rules and regulations are ignored.

The Middle Born who felt closed in by his place in the family is probably going to resent any pressure put on him, no matter where it comes from.

But if April fifteenth is just around the corner, he'd better not ignore the pressure the Internal Revenue Service has put on him. What you need, if you recognize that you are one of those free-spirited Middle Borns, is someone who will apply gentle pressure and do his or her best to keep your feet on the straight and narrow.

It's an extreme example, I know, but I recently met with a woman who made a startlingly painful discovery. Well, actually, she didn't make the discovery—the IRS did. It seems that her husband hadn't paid a cent of income tax over the last ten years. Why not? He had no explanation for what he had done, because he could have easily paid the taxes year by year. But, with penalty and interest, he now owes nearly a hundred thousand dollars, and that won't be so easy to come up with.

I have no explanation for his behavior, either, except to say that he was a Middle Born who resented any type of authority and pressure. It is too bad that he chose such a way to show his rebellion. Now his wife wishes she had stayed more on top of things and put pressure on him to do what he was supposed to do.

3. SUFFERING FROM THE "SQUEEZED-CHILD" SYNDROME

The Middle Born who resents the fact that nobody ever seemed to pay much attention to him is a "Squeezed Child."

Like most Middle Borns he may have a great many friends, but most of these relationships will be superficial. He won't trust other people enough to really open up to them. He may not even realize it, but deep down inside he has the attitude that "nobody really cares about me, so I have to look out for myself."

The one who suffers from the "Squeezed-Child" syndrome is likely to play things very close to the vest. He'll be secretive about things, and he's not likely to ask for help even when everybody else around him knows he needs it!

For that reason this Middle Child is best off in a romantic partnership with someone who is open and joyous. It may take a fun-loving Last Born to bring him out of his shell.

At the same time she would have to be patient and understand that his hesitancy to share his deepest, innermost thoughts has nothing at all to do with her. It is merely the result of his birth order and his upbringing. Being able to keep a secret is an admirable trait and can serve the Middle Child well in many areas of life. Any man or woman should appreciate having a spouse who doesn't feel a need to gossip or spill secrets.

But at the same time his tendency to avoid asking for help in any situation is more than likely going to cause some trouble.

I know that there are many things about men in general that tend to irritate the heck out of women. One of the most aggravating is that we men just hate to ask for directions.

She says, "Honey, it's obvious we're lost. Why don't you stop at that gas station over there and ask the man for directions?"

He says, "Nah—there's no need to do that. I know it's right around here somewhere."

"But we've been past this corner six times, and we're never going to get there in time."

"No, really, I know I can find it."

Well, chances are that the husband in this little drama is eventually going to have to swallow his pride, stop at the gas station, and get directions to wherever it is they're going. Only, chances are that he'll act angry about it and still insist that he could have found it without anyone's help.

That sort of behavior can be fairly typical of the Middle Born who grew up as a "Squeezed Child."

There is certainly nothing wrong with being self-sufficient and wanting to do things for yourself. The problem, though, is that you need to know when the time has come to admit that you need help.

How do you overcome the negative characteristics of the "Squeezed-Child" syndrome?

—By making the conscious decision to open yourself up to your mate, realizing that love sometimes places you in the position of being vulnerable.

—By practicing asking others for help. Borrow your neighbor's rake, stop and ask directions the next time you need to go somewhere in an unfamiliar neighborhood, and so on. If you learn how to ask for help in simple situations such as these, you'll be more apt to be able to ask for help in far more important situations.

—Remember that your spouse loves you because of who you are, not in spite of it. You are not an anonymous, faceless person, and there are people who care about you deeply.

4. FEELING INFERIOR TO OTHERS

This is true of the Middle Born whose older sibling was of the same sex and was a true overachiever. This Middle Born is likely to learn very early in life that he just can't measure up to the achievements of big brother or big sis.

That's nonsense, of course, because the Middle-Born child has his own unique strengths.

But if you are a Middle Born who is plagued with feelings of inferiority, you need the help and partnership of someone who is strong, self-assured, and who believes in you as much as he believes in himself. This probably translates out to a Firstborn, although not one who leans too far either toward being a controller or a pleaser.

An out-and-out controller would probably wind up dominating you because of your tendency to think that other people are more capable than you are. A pleaser, on the other hand, would tend to join with you in your feelings of inadequacy, and your marriage might possibly become one long-term pity party.

But the strong, confident, goal-oriented Firstborn is quite likely going to be just what the doctor ordered. Finding someone such as that who really believes in you is the first step toward learning to believe in yourself.

What you certainly don't need, if you see yourself being described here, is someone who is going to enjoy criticizing and picking on you.

If the person you are seeing has a tendency to make jokes at your expense, or to put you down constantly—even if he does it in a teasing fashion—he's the last person on earth you need, so get rid of him!

5. BEING INTENSELY LOYAL

No, there's nothing wrong with being loyal. This is something everybody wants in a partner.

The Middle Born tends to be loyal to his friends, his company, his church, his mate.

In this he differs somewhat from the Firstborn, who tends to uphold the traditions of his parents. The Middle Born is more apt to want to find his own beliefs, his own traditions. He wants to do things on his own terms, but once he has established his own relationships and his own patterns, he will be fiercely loyal.

Remember that we said the Middle Born who has felt closed in may develop into a rather rebellious and free-spirited sort of person. But even within his rebellion there often develops an allegiance to new groups, forms, and structures.

6. BEING COMPETITIVE

The Middle Born may be intensely competitive because he developed an I'll-show-you attitude.

For instance, perhaps when she was a child, she begged her mother to let her go on a bicycle outing with her big sister, but Mom said no because she was too little.

Now, she could have reacted by letting this situation make her feel inferior to her sister—since she wasn't able to do all the things sis could do—or she could have reacted by saying, "I'll show you," gotten her tricycle out of the garage, and ridden off on an adventure of her own.

If she was the type who did the latter, she probably wound up getting a spanking. But this would only have increased her determination to show everybody that she could do anything they could do. The Middle Born who is competitive in this way does not need to be married to someone who sees a marriage as a competition. Because her tendencies are so much like those of the Firstborn, she is apt to do better with a more "laid-back" Last Born who is content to let her assume the leadership role in the marriage.

Now we've explored some of the personality traits of the Middle Born and talked about the sort of person he needs to marry if he demonstrates certain of those traits—but what about the search for that particular person? Coming up next, some helpful suggestions for the Middle Born who wants to be a good romantic detective.

7

Help for the Middle-Born Romantic Detective

It was a dark and stormy night.

The lovely and innocent Miss Middle Born eyed the roomful of likely suspects.

There was Frank Firstborn, looking as if he had just stepped off the pages of *Gentleman's Quarterly*. Yes, he could be the one.

But then she couldn't rule out Mark Middle Born either. He looked like the kind of guy who could keep a secret.

And what about Larry Last Born? He looked as if he didn't have a care in the world—but you could never be too sure about what lay beneath that big smile and that easy laugh!

Miss Middle Born smiled to herself as she thought about the training she had picked up at the Leman Romantic Detective Agency.

This was going to be a piece of cake!

Okay, so maybe I'm not quite Mickey Spillane. Writing detective novels never will be my forte.

But before you're through with this chapter, I will have helped you become a romantic detective first class, whether you're a Middle Born who is in search of romance, or someone from another birth order who is seeking a romantic relationship with a Middle Born.

Now, I could spend another two hundred pages or more talking about the different types of Middle Borns, how they grow and who they ought to marry. Just think about the various combinations of children within families, and you can see what an impossible task it would be to cover all the varieties. We could talk about the fourth of six children who also is the second daughter, the first son who is the third child of seven children, et cetera. You can see how complicated it would become. But before moving on, let's take a brief look at a sample few of these various Middle-Born positions.

—A Middle-Born boy who has only brothers will be somewhat confused or ill at ease regarding his role in his family and will tend to be uncomfortable around girls and women, since there weren't any females in his immediate family. He is probably going to match up best with a free-spirited Last Born who loves life, can be somewhat of a leader within their relationship, and can thus help him overcome his natural shyness around women.

—A Middle-Born female who has only sisters will likewise be ambivalent about her expected role within the family and will tend to be rather uncomfortable around boys and men. There is no hard-and-fast rule as to which birth order matches up best with hers, but she, too, will likely do very well with a Last-Born male. However, as in all cases, if her personality has developed more along Last-Born lines, she will need to have the support and strength that would come from pairing with a Firstborn male.

—A Middle-Born male who has only sisters will tend to be seen by other men as pampered and spoiled and will generally prefer the company of women, since that's the way it always was for him at home. If it is true that his sisters have spoiled him, he will probably act more like a Last Born than a Firstborn. In most cases, though, this particular Middle Born will have no trouble relating to women. He should understand women and be sensitive to them. His ideal choice for marriage is a Firstborn female who has younger brothers or a Last-Born female with older brothers.

—A Middle-Born female who has only brothers would probably tell you that she likes men more than she does women. Being the only female is going to give her more Firstborn than Last-Born traits (since she was probably not competing directly with her older brother), and so she would be paired nicely with a Last-Born male. However, it is quite possible that she will always feel closer to her brothers than she does to her husband.

—A female with older sisters and younger brothers would tend to be submissive to females in general, but more motherly and protective with boys. Her best choice for a marriage partner is a Last-Born male who doesn't mind her motherly ways. Interestingly she is likely to be uneasy whenever she is in a situation where there are several people of both sexes, even though she would do fine with any group consisting entirely of men or entirely of women.

—A male who has older sisters and younger brothers may find it easier to relate to males on an equal basis. He may be slightly ill at ease with, or even in awe of, women, depending on how he viewed his older sister or sisters. He will match up well with the Firstborn who tends more toward being a controller than a pleaser, since that situation is where he feels most comfortable.

—A female who has older brothers and younger sisters will feel that the male should take the leadership position within a romantic relationship or marriage and will do best when paired with a goal-oriented Firstborn.

—A male who has older brothers and younger sisters is, once again, going to have a combination of both Firstborn and Last-Born traits, but when it comes to romance, he will probably feel most comfortable with a Last-Born female, since he has always related to women as a big brother.

These, then, are a few of the various combinations that work well for the Middle Born who is "looking for love."

Whereas I can't just say that every Middle Born should get involved with a Firstborn, or a Last Born, I can at least say that there are some specific traits that Middle Borns need to look for in a partner. Actually these traits are desirable in a mate no matter what your birth order may be, but they are next to necessary for the Middle Born.

The Middle Born needs to be sure that:

1. the person he is interested in will be reliable and faithful
2. the person he is interested in is honest
3. this relationship is something he really wants
4. his partner respects him and vice versa

Let's take a closer look.

1. THE MIDDLE BORN NEEDS TO BE SURE THAT THE PERSON HE IS INTERESTED IN WILL BE RELIABLE, FAITHFUL, AND HONEST

The Middle Born, as we've seen, plays it close to the vest. If you tell him a secret, he'll keep it. If you're looking for a loyal friend, look to the Middle Born. This is the sort of friend and lover he is, and it is what he needs to get back from those he loves. Betrayal or unfaithfulness, in any fashion, can be extremely hurtful for anyone, and absolutely devastating to the Middle Born.

Every woman has the right to expect her husband to be faithful to her and every man has the right to expect the same from his wife. All you have to do is listen to any couple reciting marriage vows, and you'll hear the phrase *forsaking all others.* That's not an option, it's a requisite.

I can't imagine some guy saying to his Middle-Born wife, "I'm sorry I cheated on you, Harriet, but after all I am a fun-loving Last-Born kind of guy and so it's only natural for me to be that way. I guess you'll just have to learn to live with it!"

Any man who would even consider saying such a thing ought to be forced to sit on a cholla cactus. (And those of us who live in the desert Southwest know how very painful that would be!)

I've heard some men say that it's "natural" for the male of the species to have a wandering eye, and that it's harder for a man to stay faithful to one woman than it is for a woman to stay faithful to one man. This is, of course, more baloney than the Oscar Mayer people can churn out in a good year.

I was talking once to a married military man who was bragging about how he had practically "fornicated" his way around the world.

I listened to him for a while, and then said, "And what would you do if you found out your wife was sleeping around while you were gone?"

It was as if a dark cloud suddenly descended over his face.

His smug smile was gone, replaced first by a look of utter incredulity, as if to say, *Why, she would never do anything like that!* Then that was followed almost immediately by a look of dark rage and anger. The very thought of his wife engaging in sexual activity with another man was almost more than he could take.

"Why, I'd kill him," he said. "Whoever he was, I'd kill him. I wouldn't even have to think twice about it."

He was probably telling me the truth. I've never understood why some men think it's okay for them to follow their biological urges anytime, anyplace, with anyone, but it's not okay for women to do the same thing. This worn-and-torn old double standard should have been discarded years ago. But please don't think I'm saying that if it's okay for a man to "cheat" it's okay for a woman to do the same thing. What I'm saying is that it's not okay for either of them to cheat.

I'm not suggesting that a husband or wife who's made a mistake should be tossed out on the street. I believe in forgiving and forgetting, but I don't believe that habitual and constant failure in this area should be tolerated. Furthermore, I believe that the person who is unfaithful to you in little ways while you're dating—perhaps he flirts with other women in front of you, but then insists that he's just having some "harmless" fun—is probably going to be unfaithful in more serious ways later on.

Both the husband and the wife have the right to believe that their partner will honor those marriage vows.

Any man or woman who can't seem to be faithful should be expected either to change his ways or pack his bags.

I've mentioned before that the Middle Born can keep a secret and expects others to be able to do the same for him.

If he shares a secret with you—even if it's a harmless secret that wouldn't really hurt him if it got out—you'll be wise to guard it for all you're worth. The Middle Born is fiercely loyal to those he loves and he expects the same from them.

Remember, too, that Middle Borns are the most monogamous of all birth orders. They take their promises seriously. If Joe tells Mary that she's the only one for him, he won't be dancing cheek to cheek with Veronica the next night.

Similarly, he's going to expect Mary to treat him the same way. There's no room for "romantic hypberbole" in his relationships.

Because of this it may be especially hard for the Middle Born to forgive a wandering partner.

And if you are a Middle Born who has discovered that your mate or the person you have been dating has consistently lied to you and misled you, there's no need to be "understanding." Instead it's time to say, "I'm tired of being lied to and I expect the truth from you from now on." If, after that, you still find that you're not getting the truth, it may be time for drastic action.

No, I'm not talking about buying a shotgun or hiding one of those dreaded cholla cactuses in his underwear drawer. I am talking about saying, "I'm sorry, I can't take the dishonesty anymore, and I'm going away for a few days to give us both time to think about our relationship."

Yes, you might be putting your relationship on the line. But a relationship shot full of lying and deceit isn't much of a relationship to begin with.

2. THE MIDDLE BORN NEEDS TO BE SURE THAT THIS RELATIONSHIP IS SOMETHING HE WANTS

The Middle Born, because of his tendencies to be a compromiser, is sometimes pulled into a romantic relationship by the strong will of the other person. Ask her if she really loves this guy and she might say, "Yeah, sure . . . I guess so."

If you press her, she might admit that she's not exactly over-whelmed by her feelings, but he loves her and so she'll "settle" for that. Sometimes the Middle Born might be kept in a relationship by situations and circumstances that are very far from love.

I remember Judi, for instance, who married Tom almost as soon as they graduated from high school, and much to the envy of many of the other girls in her class. Tom was a superb athlete, a tall, good-looking guy much sought after by the other girls. Unfortunately the one he wanted—Judi—didn't really want him.

They started going steady early in their senior year, but it didn't take her too long to see that he was selfish and immature. The only reason she had started going out with him in the first place was because all the other girls wanted him, and she was flattered that he was interested in her.

When she tried to break off their relationship he begged her not to. She pointed out several ways he had been inconsiderate and rude, and he promised to change if only she would give him a second chance. She gave in.

Another few weeks went by, and when she saw that he was not really interested in changing, she tried again to break up with him. This time he called her on the phone and told her he was going to kill himself because without her he had no reason to live. Frightened, she begged him not to take his life and promised that she would still be his girlfriend, if only he'd stop talking that way.

And that's the way their relationship went. She didn't really like him or respect him, she most certainly didn't love him, and yet she was afraid of what he would do to himself if she broke up with him. Even as they were sending out wedding invitations, she wondered how she had allowed herself to get caught in such a terrible trap, but she had no idea how to get out of it. She just kept hoping for a miracle, and even found herself wishing that Tom would get hit by lightning or wander into the path of a runaway freight train. But afterward she always felt terribly guilty about having such thoughts, and knew that she couldn't bear it if her actions caused him to do something harmful to himself.

By the time I came to know her she had been married to him for nearly ten years, was still feeling trapped, and still didn't know what to do. She had discovered that whenever he wanted to get his way about anything, his strategy was to put himself down or threaten himself in some way, and she would give in.

Now, as far as Judi was concerned, there were two options available to her. The first was to get her husband (and herself) into therapy and see if she could bring about a change in his behavior. The second was to walk out of the marriage and refuse to listen to any of Tom's threats.

It was too late for her to do what she should have done in the first place, and that was refuse to allow herself to be bullied into a relationship.

3. THE MIDDLE BORN NEEDS TO KNOW THAT HIS ROMANTIC PARTNER RESPECTS HIM, AND VICE VERSA

If a man and woman don't respect each other, they'll never make it through life together.

That statement cuts across all races, religions, and birth orders.

But that old "r-e-s-p-e-c-t" is especially important to the Middle Born.

Because Middle Borns are often rather anonymous members of their families—they tend to feel that nobody really respects them. The Middle Born may feel that the oldest child got all the respect, the youngest got all the coddling, and he got all the "that's nice, dears." (And to get that "that's nice, dear," just right, you've got to say it in as dull and flat a monotone as you can muster, as if there isn't really anything "nice" about it.)

"Look, Mom, I just won a Nobel prize!"

"That's nice, Leon, but your brother just got his own key to the company washroom."

"Hey, Dad, I've been given my own television special."

"Really? Did you know your sister sang a solo in church last Sunday?"

"Mom and Dad, I've just been named CEO of IBM!"

"How nice. Hey, we've got some great-looking tomatoes in our garden this year!"

Moms and dads don't mean to do that to their Middle Children, but too often this is exactly what they do!

Because of this it's extremely important for the Middle Born to be appreciated and respected by his romantic partner.

Don't overdo it. I'm not talking about flattery, but if you appreciate his wit and intelligence, tell him so.

If you admire her understanding of a difficult subject, tell her how you feel.

If her beauty takes your breath away tonight, find the words to tell her about it.

If you feel proud to be with him, let him know.

Respect is important to a Middle Born. He wants it, and he needs to have it for his partner.

Now let me say a word or two about respect in general between people involved in a romantic relationship.

Sadly, some people have grown up with a distorted view of male-female relationships and have a hard time respecting any member of the opposite sex.

Ask the man who is always looking for a conquest. All he's looking for is a little bit of sexual excitement, and he doesn't care who his partner is. It might be his wife's best friend or his best friend's wife. It's all the same to him, and if he sees an opportunity he'll go for it. He's grown up with the attitude that women are nothing more than playthings, to be used and then discarded.

There are several reasons why this sort of attitude develops. It could have been that as a young man he watched his father lording it over his mother and picked up the old man's attitude toward women. Or it could have been that he was dominated by his mother and is getting revenge by trying to dominate all the other women he comes in contact with. Whatever his reasons the man who is a womanizer does not respect women.

Oh, he respects certain "qualities" of women, all right, but let me give all the ladies a solid piece of advice: Never believe someone who tells you he respects you if he's drooling at the same time!

I've counseled many women over the years who married men they knew to have wandering eyes. They figured that once they had them signed, sealed, and delivered they'd stop their wandering ways. But it rarely works that way.

If, while he's engaged to you, you catch him ogling or flirting with other women, you'd better think twice about the relationship. Keep in mind, now, that I'm not talking about turning his head to see a pretty girl when she walks into the room. Just about every normal guy is going to do that, but there's a big difference between looking and leering!

Two questions every woman needs to ask herself about her man are "Does he respect me?" and "Does he respect women in general?"

But please don't think all the problems in this area are on the male side of the spectrum. For every womanizer, for every man who feels that women are inferior simply because they don't have testicles, there's a woman who has no respect for men.

Specifically there are women who learn pretty early in life that they can easily gain control over a man's heart and soul. They may leave a trail of broken hearts from Timbuktu to Tallahassee and never give it a second thought.

More than likely she's a "fire-and-ice" gal, who can go almost instantaneously from a burning flame to a block of ice. I've heard this one many times too: "When we were dating she just overwhelmed me with love and affection. And then, all of a sudden, she just changed. I don't know what happened."

Actually what happened is very simple. Once she caught the fish, she was no longer interested. Like her male counterpart all she was really interested in was the conquest.

"Gee, Mary Ellen, I don't know if I can believe you when you tell me how much you love me. After all, you've broken thirty-seven hearts in the last two years."

"Oh, I know, but it's different with you, Ralph. I've never felt about anyone like I feel about you."

Poor Ralph. He ought to remember what George Santayana said, that anyone who forgets history is condemned to relive it. He's about to be broken heart number thirty-eight, and he ought to bail out quickly.

You see, a marriage won't work without mutual respect, and neither will any other sort of relationship.

No matter how much of a compromiser she or he may be, the Middle Born must never, ever settle for someone whom he doesn't respect, or who doesn't respect him.

Lesson from the Middle Born

We can all learn from the Middle Born's desire and tendency to "work things out." That is the reason his marriage is able to make it over obstacles that would have totally destroyed other relationships.

This is an attitude that all couples should have: "Whatever happens, we will be able to work things out between us."

Lovers can learn many things from one another if they will keep a spirit of adventure, a willingness to try new approaches to life, and, most of all, if they will do everything they do in a spirit of love.

It's like the Beatles said twenty-five years ago: "You can work it out!"

I'm sure you've heard the old saying, but it's true that you can catch more flies with honey than you can with vinegar. You know, the reason some of these sayings have stayed around for so many years is because they have been tried and tested and found to be true.

I heard a story about a woman who had just moved to a small town. She was particularly upset by the service she received upon her visit to a neighborhood pharmacy. The pharmacist was slow, he overcharged her, and he was not friendly.

Later on, the woman confided to one of her new friends about the terrible treatment she had received in this pharmacy.

"I really feel like going down there and giving him a piece of my mind," she said, referring to the pharmacist, who also owned the little store. "If his wasn't the only drugstore in town, you can bet I'd never shop there again!"

Her friend said, "Well, I know him pretty well. Why don't you let me talk to him for you."

Several days later the newcomer had the opportunity to go back into the little drugstore. This time things were completely different. The pharmacist was efficient, friendly, and had her prescription filled in a matter of moments.

She was pleased and amazed at the turnaround in attitude and service, and as soon as she got home she telephoned her friend and thanked her. "I guess you told him how upset I was, right?"

"Well . . . I talked to him for you."

"And you told him that if he didn't do a better job the next time I came into his store, I'd never come in again?"

"Actually, no. I told him that you really liked his store, and that you appreciated the friendly service you got there."

"You told him *what?*"

"Don't be upset. It had the desired effect, didn't it?"

That it did. It is amazing what you can accomplish within yourself and in the lives of others when you're operating in a spirit of love.

The Middle Born Within a Relationship

Just as we did earlier with the Firstborn, we're going to take a look at how the Middle Born can be expected to act in the various "departments" of a marriage or relationship.

1. AT WORK

His birth-order position has given the Middle Born skill in dealing with other people, and this should serve him well within his chosen occupation. He is probably capable of getting along both with his superiors and with those who report to him. He is able to use his negotiating skills to great advantage and for this reason makes an especially effective middle manager. But that's not where the corporate ladder stops for the Middle Born. Because he or she is so adept at negotiation, compromise, and because he understands the necessity of giving something to get something, Middle Borns can do very well indeed in the corporate world.

The Middle Born is rarely a workaholic, but that doesn't mean he takes it easy with regard to his job. He will work long hours if necessary, but he generally has a balanced approach to life that won't allow him to spend all of his time working at the expense of his family. Because he tends to be a people person, his interpersonal relationships are just as important to him as his career.

2. DURING HIS LEISURE TIME

The Middle Born is not likely to be the type to hike up into the mountains so he can spend a weekend alone with his thoughts.

Oh, he might take a hike like that, but if he does, you can be pretty sure that he'll invite several friends to go along with him.

It's more likely that you'll find the Middle Born attending a meeting of a sorority or fraternal organization. If he belongs to a particular group, such as the Rotary Club, for example, he is probably going to be very active and loyal to that group. To some extent he probably tends to define himself as a member of that certain group, since he always felt somewhat anonymous and "Brand X" as a Middle-Born child.

If you're married to a Middle Born, she'll probably enjoy having people in for dinner and going to social gatherings and parties. The one drawback to this is that she's likely to have a social calendar that's too full for her own good, and for this reason her social life can begin to drag her down. He or she will sometimes wonder where the weekend went, for instance, and might be heard to mutter on a Monday morning, "I'm glad the weekend's over so I can finally get some rest."

3. DEALING WITH FINANCES

When it comes to handling money, the Middle Born is capable of doing an excellent job.

He is not as ambitious and goal oriented as his Firstborn brother or sister might be, but neither is he likely to spend money freely and compulsively as a Last Born might do. Generally, the Middle Born will set financial goals that are reasonable and accessible. He doesn't live for money. He doesn't care if he ever gets rich, just as long as he's "comfortable."

He's not stingy, and he's willing to spend money on himself and others. He's the sort of person, in fact, who will give you the proverbial shirt off his back—and maybe even the real shirt too. On the other hand he is prone to counting the cost and is not the sort of person to go deeply into debt. He doesn't believe in spending money he doesn't really have.

4. IN HIS SOCIAL RELATIONSHIPS

We've already talked about this when we addressed the way the Middle Born is probably going to spend his leisure time.

Ask a Middle Born to name his friends, and he'll probably go on for five minutes, and then remember later that he still hasn't named everyone he considers a "close" friend. The truth is, though, that most of these friends are not much more than casual acquaintances. That's because the Middle Born meets people and makes friends easily. But again, because he is so secretive and hesitant to share his innermost thoughts and feelings, he probably doesn't know all these friends very well.

You might see him at the party, carrying on an animated conversation with one or two people, and conclude that they are all the best of friends. But if you move in closer and listen to what they're saying, you'll find that they're probably talking about sports, or movies, or something equally superficial. They may even be talking about what needs to be done to make the world a better place, but even here the Middle Born is not likely to be revealing anything of his innermost feelings.

Some people may see his lack of "openness" as being cold or rude, but it's nothing more than the natural result of his birth-order position.

If you're married to a Middle Born, you're probably going to find yourself in the middle of the social whirl. You'll also find that he can be friendly and extremely outgoing—but don't expect him to want to "share" with you at a moment's notice. Yes, he can learn to open himself up, but it's not going to come without a lot of loving patience on his partner's part.

5. IN THE BEDROOM

The Middle Born can be an excellent lover. He or she will be concerned about his partner's desires and feelings, but not to the point where he'll forget about his own needs.

In other words he or she understands the give-and-take that is necessary to turn "having sex" into "making love."

The one possible drawback, when it comes to the area of sex, is that the Middle Born might be hesitant to tell his partner what he really wants or likes. This is another area where he might play it a little bit closer to the vest than is necessary.

For instance, a Middle-Born male might hesitate to tell his wife when he's in the mood for making love, because he doesn't want to be seen as too aggressive or do anything she doesn't want him to do—and what if she doesn't feel like it? He may desperately want his partner to "make the first move" but won't do anything to let her know that's how he feels.

For this reason he needs a partner who can be patient, loving, and perceptive.

But once you and your Middle-Born spouse get to know each other's sexual likes, dislikes, and special passions—you're going to be tremendous bed partners.

6. IN PARENTING

Remember what I said earlier, that every parent tends to overidentify with the child who occupies his own birth-order position.

Beyond that the Middle-Born parent is more likely to see his child's point of view than other birth-order parents would be. As in "Well, I can see that you disobeyed me, but after talking to you about what you did I see that you weren't so sure about the rule—so I suppose I won't punish you this time." The Middle Born is thus more likely to be a compromiser than a strict disciplinarian.

Now, being able to see the child's point of view is good, and being able to admit to a child that you made a mistake and are sorry is healthy for parent-child relationships. But not being able to stick to your guns when it comes to discipline is bad, because children need to know what the rules are and what their punishment is going to be if they don't follow those rules. If the parent is very angry about something one day and then laughs the same thing off the next day, the child will never know how he has to behave and he'll always be testing the limits, seeing how much he can get away with.

Parents must be evenhanded and firm in the disciplining of their children. If you are married to a Middle Born, you must have a firm agreement as to how you will administer discipline, and then stick to it.

The old wisdom says that having children can help to put a troubled marriage back together. But I'm here to tell you that having children can also tear a good marriage apart. Especially if the parents haven't come to an agreement on how to handle disciplinary matters. And if you think you're not going to have discipline problems of one sort or another, I know some choice Florida swampland I'd like to sell you.

7. WHEN IT COMES TO STRESS

Middle Borns are less worried and anxious than their older brothers or sisters. Part of the reason may be that their parents were less worried and anxious as they went through various stages of their development.

For instance, the First Born's first day of school is likely to turn Mom and Dad both into nervous wrecks. Will he be okay? Will he get along with the other kids? Will the teacher be nice to him? What if he loses his milk money? And so on. But by the time the Middle Born goes off to school, it's no big deal. When the First Born gets his first ear infection or fever, his parents are in a state of near panic. But when it happens to their next child, they know exactly what to do.

Furthermore, Mom and Dad put much more pressure to perform on the First Born than they did on their next child. For that reason he's not as driven, as goal oriented, or as likely to be stressed out.

The Middle Born's ability to compromise also serves him well in this area. He realizes that give-and-take is a natural part of life, and he doesn't get into a lather if everything doesn't go his way.

There is one particular problem for the Middle Born, and that is that he is not likely to seek help or admit he needs it. When the Firstborn feels overwhelmed by stress, he's probably going to seek out the help of a competent therapist. The Middle Born, on the other hand, will deny that he has a problem.

In other words the Middle Born is not nearly as likely to be troubled by stress as his older brother or sister—but if he should become stressed out he may let the problem become quite severe before he attempts to deal with it.

8 . IN RELIGION AND PHILOSOPHY

If you are going to marry a Middle Born, you are going to marry someone who is likely to have a strongly defined list of philosophical and religious beliefs. But those beliefs are not necessarily going to be the same ones that were held by his parents, and he's not going to be the sort who naturally wants to share those beliefs with others.

If the person who comes to you and wants to tell you about his religion is a Middle Born, you can bet he feels very deeply about what he believes. It's taken a great deal of passion to get him to overcome his natural tendency to keep his deepest beliefs and feelings to himself. The Middle Born is more likely to be the type who'll say, "I think religion is a very personal matter." He'll be offended by celebrities and politicians who tend to be loudly outspoken about their beliefs, and he'll be a bit suspicious of their motives too.

Middle Borns resent other people making their decisions for them. They want to figure things out for themselves.

One strongly Orthodox Jewish family was astonished when their Middle-Born son came home from college and told them that he had converted to Christianity. They couldn't understand how he could do something that they saw as a betrayal of their heritage. It wasn't easy, but after a while the parents were able to accept their son's newfound faith—not for themselves, but as an expression of their son's desire to find his own place in the world.

The passionate convert, whether to Christianity from Judaism, to Judaism from Christianity, or to the Lutheran Church from the Methodist Church, is much more likely to be a Middle Born. He is saying, in effect, "I am not content with being an anonymous face that goes along with the crowd. I am somebody unique, and I will find my own way in life."

What Keeps a Marriage Going?

Psychology Today magazine interviewed 351 couples who had been married for fifteen years or more to find out why their marriages had lasted so long.[1] Of the 351 couples surveyed, 300 said they were happily married, 19 said they were unhappy but were staying together for other reasons, and in 32 cases only one of the partners said he or she was not happy in the marriage.

The couples were given a variety of reasons why marriages last and told to choose the ones that applied most directly to their marriages. Here are the top reasons why these marriages had lasted so long. I present them without comment, except to say that it is interesting and revealing how similar the men's and women's choices are. First, the women's responses, and then the men's:

WOMEN

1. My spouse is my best friend.
2. I like my spouse as a person.
3. Marriage is a long-term commitment.
4. Marriage is sacred.
5. We agree on aims and goals.
6. My spouse has grown more interesting.
7. I want the relationship to succeed.
8. We laugh together.
9. We agree on a philosophy of life.
10. We agree on how and how often to show affection.

MEN

1. My spouse is my best friend.
2. I like my spouse as a person.
3. Marriage is a long-term commitment.
4. Marriage is sacred.
5. We agree on aims and goals.
6. My spouse has grown more interesting.
7. I want the relationship to succeed.
8. An enduring marriage is important to social stability.
9. We laugh together.
10. I am proud of my spouse's achievements.

PART FOUR

For Last Borns Only

8

Loose-Living Last Borns: Having a Ball on the Road to Disaster

Okay, Last Born, before I go any farther, I've got to let you know that I'm wise to you.

I know you're just starting the book here. But that's okay, because I wouldn't expect anything else from a Last Born. And who knows? Maybe next summer you'll find the time to read the whole thing.

In this chapter we're going to take a look at what happens when two Last Borns wind up in love with each other. Then, in the following chapter, we'll take a look at the very best romantic matches for the Last Born. And, finally, just as we've done for the Firstborns and Middle Borns, we'll follow that up with some special tips for the Last-Born romantic detective.

I want to remind you again that if I seem a little bit harsh in my judgment of Last Borns, that's only because I am one. So if you're a Last Born, remember that I'm talking to myself here as much as I am talking to you.

As a matter of fact I just had a rather embarrassing experience that reminded me of the way we Last Borns can sometimes concentrate on the fun and games and leave the more important things undone.

You see, I take great pride in being a good father. I think by almost any standard you'd find that I grade out to an A or even an A-plus. As far as I'm concerned, being a good parent is the most important thing anyone could ever be, and I take the job seriously.

Keeping that in mind, here's the story.

My wife recently took a two-day trip to Phoenix. She needed a little R and R and took our oldest daughter, Holly, along with her. The two of them planned to do some shopping, take in a movie or two, and just enjoy their time together. That left me at home in Tucson with Kevin, Krissy, and little Hannah, who is two and a half years old.

After the first night the older two found refuge at their friends' homes and left Hannah and me alone. Well, Sande called that first evening and gave me the third degree worthy of a hardened police sergeant. How were we getting along? What were the kids up to? And on and on. I reassured her that things were fine, that I was in perfect control of the situation, and told her to stop worrying.

The second night she called again and asked me about the day we had had.

I told her about all the fun things we had done, the stories we read, the games we had played, et cetera.

Then she said, "What did you feed her for lunch?"

All of a sudden there was dead silence on my end of the phone.

Lunch? Er . . . I knew I'd forgotten something.

I had forgotten to feed my daughter.

Oh, I had given her breakfast—an egg and some toast—and I'd given her a bottle when I put her to bed, but nothing else the rest of the day.

The day was awfully hectic and somehow, in the rush, I simply forgot.

Sande and I have had several good laughs over this incident. She knows that sometimes we babies just forget.

And, once again I am left feeling very grateful for my on-top-of-things Firstborn wife.

Let me tell you up front, before we go any farther, that a marriage between two Last Borns is likely to be a pretty wild ride. If you don't like roller coasters, maybe you'd better pass this chapter altogether!

What are the major problem areas for a couple of Last Borns?

1. They love the idea of play now, pay later.
2. They love being pampered and spoiled.
3. They're likely to zig when they ought to zag.
4. They both crave the spotlight.
5. They may be jealous of their older siblings.

I'd say that their desire to play now, pay later is one of the biggest problems. You see, if a couple of Last Borns have to choose between having a good time and being responsible, you can almost be sure that they're going to choose the good time. They're not the sort of people who will worry overly much about the consequences. The attitude is "We'll take care of tomorrow when tomorrow gets here."

A Last Born is a wonderful balance to the always-serious Firstborn. The Last Born shows the Firstborn that life is not always deadly serious and that it's okay to have some laughs now and then. The Firstborn, on the other hand, will help the Last Born to face up to responsibility, showing him that there are times when life is serious indeed, and it has to be treated that way. In this way they form a good team, and the two of them are able to have a balanced approach to life.

But put two Last Borns together and they are likely to feed on each other's sense of fun and excitement.

They may be walking through the mall when one of them sees a fancy new brass bed sitting in the window of a furniture store.

The wife says, "Hey, isn't that nice. That would really look great in our bedroom."

The husband says, "You're right. Let's get it!" The thing may cost a fortune, and they may not really be able to afford it, but they won't stop to think about those things.

Then they'll go into a department store, and he'll see a suit he likes. He doesn't really need another suit, but what the heck, it would never hurt to have another one, and his fun-loving wife isn't going to tell him he doesn't need it. Then it's over to the kitchen appliances, where there's this new combination food-processor and coffee maker. And so it goes, as they spend themselves into oblivion.

But chances are that if one of them had not been a Last Born, the spending spree never would have happened.

The husband might have said, "Yes, that is a beautiful brass bed. It's too bad we can't afford it right now."

Or the wife might have told her Last-Born husband, "That's a nice-looking suit, hon, but you have several suits hanging in the closet at home. I really don't think you need to get another one right now."

The Last-Born spouse might not have enjoyed hearing that sort of negative talk and might have been reluctant to listen. He might have become angry because his wife "wouldn't let him" buy that new suit, but he would be much better off because of her more sensible approach to life.

1. THEY LOVE THE IDEA OF PLAY NOW, PAY LATER

I have been working with a typical pair of Last Borns. Their names are Ted and Alice, and their inability to plan for the future has put their marriage on a rocky footing.

It all started when the two of them had a chance to buy one of the nicest houses in their neighborhood. The owner had been transferred to another state and was anxious to sell. So anxious, in fact, that he was selling the house for fifteen thousand dollars less than its appraised value. He was asking only five thousand to assume his loan, and that meant anyone who bought the house would be starting out with ten thousand dollars in equity. Another thing about this deal that made it especially appealing to Ted and Alice was that because the house was an assumption, there was no need to qualify.

They both knew that they would have had a hard time qualify-
ing, since they had often found themselves in financial trouble in
the past. Ted and Alice had always been Last Borns through and
through. Whatever they saw that they wanted, they bought. It
didn't seem that they had ever heard of the idea that you could
save up to buy something, or that you could put something on
layaway and then take it home after you had paid for it. When
they wanted something, whatever it was, they wanted it now. The
result had always been a number of charge cards that were near or
over the limit, phone calls from collection agencies, and credit
being cut off.

This time, though, things were going to be different. This house
was so big and roomy, it was the dream house both of them had
always wanted. There was just one catch, though, and that was
that they couldn't really afford to make the payments.

Certainly a small oversight. Nothing worth losing sleep over.

Over lunch one day one of Ted's co-workers had even tried to
talk to him about the wisdom of buying the house:

"Aren't you worried about making those big payments?"

"No, not at all."

"I don't know, Ted. That's a lot of money, and unless you're
making a lot more than I am . . ."

"I'm not worried about it."

That was the end of the conversation.

After Ted and Alice moved into their new home, they didn't
have any trouble at all making the payments—for the first two
months. By the third month they were faced with a dilemma. If
they paid the mortgage, they wouldn't be able to pay both the
phone bill and the electric bill. They opted to let the phone bill go,
figuring that having electric power was more necessary than having a telephone. They figured they'd catch up on the phone bill the
following month, although how they thought they were going to
do that was anybody's guess.

In the meantime neither of them had made any changes in life-
style. Ted was going out to lunch five days a week and wouldn't
even consider brown-bagging it. Alice, for her part, wouldn't give

up her once-weekly dinners with her friends. And even when her friends suggested that they cut back and go to restaurants that were a little less expensive, she wouldn't hear of it. She said that she wasn't going to spend her evening out with the girls eating burgers and fries.

When one of their neighbor's daughters was married, Ted and Alice went out and bought an expensive silver service as a wedding present.

"We had to do something nice," Alice said. "After all, we've known the people for a long time, and we couldn't very well give their daughter some towels or something like that." My response to that as a psychologist is "Why not?"—because you can only do what you can afford. My response as a Last Born is to be sympathetic and understand, because I fight those tendencies to overdo it in the spending department myself. Fortunately, though, I am married to a Firstborn, and Sande is always there to talk some sense into me before I get too deeply into the quicksand. Ted and Alice, it seems, were urging each other to go farther out into the quicksand, instead of helping pull each other out of it.

Things really began to get bad the fourth month they were in their new house; it was November, and time to start buying presents for Christmas. They were faced with a terrible dilemma, because they couldn't afford to pay the mortgage and buy Christmas presents for their friends and family. The telephone had long since been disconnected, they had had to borrow money from friends to get their water turned back on, and they were already getting unpleasant letters from the electric company.

They decided that the only thing they could do was let the mortgage go. If they did that, they'd be able to catch up on the electric bill, pay the phone bill, and then have enough left to give their kids a good Christmas.

And a whale of a Christmas it was too!

Sadly enough they didn't seem to be learning from any of their mistakes. There was no long-term planning. Instead there was an attitude of "Let's live for today," and their attention was always given to finding ways to get out of the immediate situation. Never did they sit down and draw up a plan to help them avoid problems in the future.

They are so deep in the hole now that neither of them knows what's going to happen next. Both of them seem to have changed personalities. They're so serious and solemn that you'd think they were a couple of Super Firstborns.

But their Last-Born personality patterns are so deeply ingrained that I wonder if they wouldn't return to their free-spending ways at the first opportunity.

The story I've told you has been pieced together from the accounts both of them have given me. But if I were to report the story to you the way Alice gave it to me, you'd see that the whole mess was Ted's fault. On the other hand, Ted's accounts point the finger of blame directly at his wife.

This is another hallmark of Last Borns. They're great when it comes to passing the buck or blaming someone else.

Right about now some Last-Born reader is probably saying, "Hey, Leman, you're cruising for a fat lip! How dare you say so many harsh things about Last Borns?" Well, again, let me remind you that I am a Last Born myself, so I know what I'm talking about!

I'm not going to invite you over to my house to look at my credit-card bills. I'd be too embarrassed to have you see them. But how grateful I am to be married to a sensible Firstborn who will never grant me enough rope to hang myself. I hate to think of the predicament I could be in if I were left to my own devices, or if I had a wife who encouraged me in my irresponsible tendencies.

Please bear in mind, it's not that Last Borns don't have any good qualities. The truth is that we babies have a great number of terrific traits. But those traits tend to go unnoticed when two Last Borns team up. That's because they tend to multiply each other's weaknesses. And please remember that in this particular chapter, I am talking about the specific problems that can arise when two Last Borns combine forces.

A romantic relationship between two people of the same birth order can be a lot like taking an overdose of medicine. What I mean is that most medicines have some unpleasant side effects. If you take more of a particular medicine than has been prescribed, it won't increase the benefits of the medicine, but it will increase the side effects. So, take one perfectly wonderful Last Born whose only vice is that he's a compulsive spender, and team him up with a financially responsible Firstborn, and no problem. But take two perfectly wonderful Last Borns, who both have the same compulsive spending problem, team them up—and watch out!

2. THEY LOVE BEING PAMPERED AND SPOILED

Have you ever known anyone who couldn't seem to do anything for himself? It's not that he didn't have the ability—he just didn't have the inclination. You might have laughed about him and said, "He should have been a king, because he sure doesn't mind letting other people wait on him."

Chances are good that you nodded your head yes when I asked if you know a person like that. Just about everyone does.

If you know a little king or queen, it's likely that he or she is a Last Born. It makes sense, first of all, because parents tend to let the Last Borns be babies long past the time when the other children were expected to "act your age."

You see, when the baby came along, all of a sudden all the other children in the family were seen as little adults whether they were or not. All of Mom's attention (and Dad's too) was directed at little Mortimer, and in most instances the others were expected to fend for themselves.

"Mom, what's for breakfast?" asks Maximilian, who is six.

"Honey, there's cereal under the counter and there's milk in the refrigerator. You're a big boy now, so go ahead and help yourself."

Mom isn't trying to be mean to Max, but she has her hands full with baby Mortimer right now and doesn't have time to take care of the others in the same way that she used to.

Unfortunately, as the years go by, the parents will more than likely continue doting on Mortimer. It's not that they love him more, but the perspective shifts so that they always see him as the baby, the one who needs special assistance, and the others are always seen as more grown up and capable of taking care of themselves.

Because of this, Mortimer becomes accustomed to having other people wait on him.

But it isn't only Mom and Dad who instill in him the belief that he deserves to be waited on. His big brothers and sisters do it too.

What happens when Mortimer is thirsty?

"Mom, Mortimer wants a drink."

"Mom, Mortimer's hungry."

"Dad, Mortimer has to go to the bathroom."

I have seen cases where Last-Born children were delayed in verbal development because older brothers and sisters did all of their talking for them. Why should the child bother to speak when he never has to? Parents would come in to see me, frantically worried that something was wrong with Last Born's mental development because he just wasn't saying anything. A closer investigation revealed that the child was actually brilliant. He wasn't about to do anything that hampered his chances of having his every need met by solicitous brothers and sisters—and that included learning to talk for himself!

Is a bully picking on little Mort? He won't do it for long, because big brother's going to take care of him.

Is there a project at school that Mort just can't seem to do? Chances are good that Sis will take him in hand and show him how it's done. More than likely she'll even go ahead and do it for him.

And so life goes for the Last Born.

Unfortunately, unless you really are a little prince or princess, this sort of life doesn't last very long. Sooner or later you're on your own in the world, and then you don't have big brothers and sisters, or doting parents, to see that every need is met. That's when you have to start doing things for yourself.

The woman who has grown up in this fashion may expect her husband to wait on her constantly. If her husband is a Last Born, though, he may expect his wife to treat him just the way his Mom did.

The result is going to be two people who are angry and disappointed and who don't understand how their spouses could be so selfish. Both of them, you see, have misunderstood the concept of marriage as an equal relationship in which each partner does his best to make the other happy. He wasn't looking for a wife, he was looking for a maid. She wasn't looking for a husband, she was looking for a sugar daddy.

Unless both of them realize that you get out of a relationship only what you put into it, the marriage is headed for disaster. One such Last-Born husband told me, "I know I'm selfish, but I've been that way for so long that it's hard to change."

My response to him was that he'd better change, and soon, if he wanted to save his marriage. Fortunately he did. Unfortunately the tendency of the Last Born is to say, "I'll change if you'll change." And so the Last-Born couple goes through life, neither one ever changing a thing!

3. THEY'RE LIKELY TO ZIG WHEN THEY OUGHT TO ZAG

When I was a kid, growing up in Williamsville, New York, I used to spend quite a bit of time out on the water, either boating or fishing. I loved being out on the water when I was a boy, and I still love it today.

But I will never forget the first time I took a rowboat out onto a lake. I insisted I knew how to row it. (That's another thing about Last Borns. We don't think we need lessons or instructions.) How embarrassed I was when I couldn't get that little boat to go straight to save my life. I knew very well that I was doing everything necessary to make that boat go straight, but it just wouldn't do it. It insisted in going in circles for the first fifteen minutes. Once I got out of that pattern I went this way, then that way, then this way again—much to my own consternation and the hilarity of those onshore who were watching my first effort as "ship's captain."

Well, two Last Borns will sometimes go through life as if they were riding in that little boat. They may have a particular destination in mind, but from watching them you'd never know where they were going.

The Last Born is not the sort of person to stick to a steady course, nor is he likely to hold out until the bitter end.

If Joe Last Born is married to someone who understands his nature, who will perhaps sympathize with him, massage his ego a bit, and urge him to continue on, he'll be fine.

But let him team up with someone who shares his compulsive tendencies or his desire to make one good deal pay off handsomely, and both of them could be in trouble.

For example, he has a bad day at work.

"Honey," he says, as he comes through the door at the end of the day, "I've had it with that stupid job of mine. The boss is a jerk, he doesn't appreciate me, and I'm wasting my talents there anyway. I'm going to quit!"

Last-Born wife says, "You're absolutely right. I don't know how you've stuck it out this long. You call that miserable old coot right now and tell him that you quit."

So that's exactly what he does.

Later on he may totally regret his action. But because he didn't have someone to calm him down and get him to really think about his actions, he followed through on his impulses.

One Last-Born acquaintance has had at least six jobs over the past three years. He never stays very long in any one place because he gets fed up and decides, "I'm never gonna get anywhere in this crummy job." Well, if you stay in a job for six months or less, that's hardly enough time to work your way up to vice-president.

My friend, Rodney, is always looking for the big score. He's a dreamer and a schemer, and it's particularly sad because he's in his forties now and it's time he knew better. As for his wife, she dreams and schemes right along with him.

I'm afraid that one day they will both be sixty-five but with no investments, no pension, no money to retire on.

And this is what I mean by saying that Last Borns are likely to zig when they ought to zag. They can be capricious and willful and make complete changes in their lives without really thinking ahead to consider the consequences of their actions.

Before moving on I want to make sure that I don't leave the impression that the Last Born may zig and zag all over the place because he's greedy. That may be the case, but it's just as likely that he's seeking some other elusive goal. Perhaps he doesn't find that his job is fulfilling. His motives could even be altruistic—perhaps he's always looking for a place where he can be of more service to people. (Last Borns are extremely people oriented, after all.) But whatever his motivations may be, the problem is that he may make impulsive decisions that will ultimately prove to be harmful.

He needs someone to rein him in, and not a partner who is going to be urging him to "go with the flow."

4. THEY BOTH CRAVE THE SPOTLIGHT

From the time Little Jake was born, it's been, "Oh, isn't he cute?" Big brother probably had to take his little brother along on a date or two, and then sat steaming while his girlfriend oohed and ahhed over his sweet little brother.

If Jake did something that would have been considered rude and obnoxious if older brother had done it, people smiled and laughed and talked about how adorable he was.

Last Borns generally have oodles of attention as they're growing up, and they enjoy every minute of it.

But put two spotlight-hogging Last Borns together, and you're bound to have trouble.

Chances are that a union of two people like that will resemble *Star Search* more than it will a marriage.

And it's obvious that a marriage isn't going to work when each person is jealous of the attention the other one gets.

The man in such a marriage has to learn that it's a good thing when his wife is in the limelight. He needs to let her shine and sparkle and be the center of attention on occasion. The wife needs to learn, on the other hand, that she can fade into the background once in a while and let her husband be the life of the party.

5. THEY MAY BE JEALOUS OF THEIR OLDER SIBLINGS

Well, why shouldn't we babies be jealous of our older brothers and sisters?

I mean, when we were little, we had to stay at home while we watched our lucky siblings go off to school. They got all sorts of privileges we couldn't get because we were "too little," like staying up later at night.

We can remember lying in bed when we were kids and feeling jealous because the sound from the TV set was coming through the walls and we knew our older brothers and sisters were getting to enjoy the best program in the whole world. Maybe we didn't even know what it was, but we knew it was stupendous, simply because we were missing it and they weren't.

These were some of the drawbacks that grew out of being the baby of the family. And, whether it is unfortunate or fortunate depends upon the situation, but the truth is that once you're the baby, you're always the baby. You might grow up to be six four and 265 pounds, but you're still going to be the baby.

The person who is jealous of his older siblings is going to go to great lengths to outdo them, to prove he's better than they are. And if that's your primary motivation, it makes for a rough time in life.

People who are jealous tend to be suspicious of others' motives and actions, angry at what they perceive to be the undeserved good fortune of others. Team two such people up and they're probably going to feed each other's paranoia—and that won't make for a good marriage. In Chapter Two I talked about how two hard-driving Firstborns can turn a marriage into a track meet. Well, two

BEST MARRIAGE MATCHUPS
FOR LAST BORNS

   +

LAST-BORN MALE   **PLUS**   **FIRSTBORN FEMALE**
WITH OLDER BROTHERS   **WITH YOUNGER BROTHERS**

   +

LAST-BORN FEMALE   **PLUS**   **FIRSTBORN MALE**
WITH OLDER BROTHERS   **WITH YOUNGER SISTERS**

   +

LAST-BORN MALE   **PLUS**   **FIRSTBORN FEMALE**
WITH OLDER SISTERS   **WITH YOUNGER SISTERS**

   +

LAST-BORN FEMALE   **PLUS**   **FIRSTBORN MALE**
WITH OLDER SISTERS   **WITH YOUNGER SISTERS**

LAST-BORN FEMALE   PLUS   **FIRSTBORN MALE**
WITH OLDER BROTHERS   **WITH YOUNGER BROTHERS**
AND SISTERS   **AND SISTERS**

LAST-BORN MALE   PLUS   **FIRSTBORN FEMALE**
WITH OLDER BROTHERS   **WITH YOUNGER BROTHERS**
AND SISTERS   **AND SISTERS**

Last Borns who are jealous of their older siblings can do the same thing. The only difference is that the Last Borns probably won't seek to outdo their siblings through hard work and perseverance. They'll look to prove their worth through that "one big moment" in the spotlight, but they angle and work for that moment for years.

Babies need to remember that there's nothing at all wrong with being the Last Born or being designated as the baby of the family. Understanding that ought to help assuage the jealousy they feel, but I am aware that some Last Borns bristle at the thought of being called "babies."

A young man named Larry, who is a student at Purdue University, wrote me an indignant letter in which he said:

> I am the youngest in my family and find it disturbing that you refer to the Last Born as "the baby in the family." Calling the Last Borns "babies" continues the negative stereotypes people use when referring to the Last Born—such negative stereotypes as being inept, not as smart as brothers or sisters, not man

enough in certain situations, being shy, unprofessional behavior, not having the right stuff for leadership, et cetera.

Dr. Leman, you as a nationally known psychologist should know better than to insult other people's pride and self-esteem.

Finally, Larry writes, "I have noted many times in the past that if I tell someone I am the Last Born they automatically switch gears and treat me condescendingly without respect."

Does it sound a little bit to you as if Larry might be carrying around some resentment toward his older siblings? It does to me.

And all I can say to Larry, and to other Last Borns who feel the way he does, is that it has never been my intention to say that one birth position is better, or worse, than any other. However, each birth position has inherent strengths and weaknesses, and the Last Born's weaknesses stem primarily from his position as the pampered and spoiled "baby" of the family.

Overcoming Your Last-Born Tendencies

What can you do if you are a Last Born who is married to another Last Born, and if you recognize yourself in some of the marriages we've discussed in this chapter?

There are several steps you can take to improve your marriage.

—First of all, if you recognize that you have selfish tendencies, you can do something for your spouse without expecting to be given anything in return. It doesn't have to be anything terribly difficult or expensive. Surprise her with a small bouquet of flowers delivered to the house. Send a mushy card to him at the office. Tell her you're going to watch the kids for an evening so she can go out with some of her friends. Ship the kids off to a sitter and prepare his favorite dinner. In these ways you're learning to do things for each other. The more you practice focusing on the needs of others, the easier it will be.

—Next, you can ask another of your family members or friends to tell you about his feelings and plans. Learning to care about others is a good way to submerge your own selfish tendencies and thus be better prepared to deal with those tendencies in your mate.

—You can also accept the fact that there are some times when you will be relegated to the back burner. You do not always have to have the spotlight. You won't always be noticed, and you need to learn to be content to stay in the background every once in a while.

—You can also learn to control your spending. You don't have to have everything you want. Besides that, if you save up for something, it will mean more when you can actually go and bring it home from the store. If you learn to exercise discipline when it comes to finances, you will have discipline in other areas of your life as well.

—You can learn not to follow your feelings all the time. Stick to that steady course, remembering that it will pay off in the end.

—You and your spouse can make a list of all the good things that came your way specifically because you were the babies of the family.

—Finally, you can see to it that your spouse is held accountable for his actions. If you have done everything you can do to hold your "free-spending, spotlight-hugging" tendencies in check, you can ask and expect him to do the same thing.

Are you a Last Born who is thinking seriously about marrying another Last Born? I wouldn't be the one to tell you not to do it. But before you do, let me have you do one thing. Take a good long look at your bank account, and the bank account of the person you're going to marry.

Is one of you rich? If so, that's very good. If you're going to be supporting two Last-Born spending habits, you're probably going to need all the money you can get!

9

The Last Born and His Perfect Match

Imagine this scene:

You're trying to watch the late-night movie, *Plan Nine from Outer Space,* or something equally bizarre. But it's frustrating, because every time the action gets the least bit exciting, they cut for a commercial, and there *he* is again.

"Folks," he says, "come on down to Crazie Charlie's used-car lot, just next to the freeway overpass! We've got red cars, blue cars, green cars—we've got Fords, Chevrolets, and Plymouths—you name it, we've got it. . . ." On and on he goes, and you wonder how he can talk so fast and say so much in between breaths.

In one commercial he may be riding an ostrich or a camel; in the next one he's walking on his hands or sticking his head in a lion's mouth. Most often he's pounding on the hood of some old wreck and telling you that you won't find a better deal anywhere else within the free world. And all of this just because he wants to sell you a used car.

I'll tell you something about this fellow: He's a Last Born to the nth degree!

But have you ever wondered what kind of a woman is married to this guy?

She must be one heck of a gal, that's for sure! I mean, can you imagine dealing with this hyperactive ball of zany energy day after day after day?

Looking at this guy on TV you probably get a quick idea of what she must be like:

Platinum-blond hair—but don't look too close or you'll see the dark roots—a squeaky voice, enough makeup to keep a fleet of Mary Kay saleswomen in pink Cadillacs, probably hasn't read a book since high school (assuming, that is, she actually read one then), forty-seven pounds of gaudy jewelry on her hands and hanging around her neck—and she probably can't walk down the aisle of the local supermarket without knocking a bunch of things off the shelves with her swinging hips.

Is that what you see? Well, I for one will bet that this picture is way off base.

Let me tell you what his wife is probably really like.

1. She has a calm, no-nonsense approach to life. She's not easily rattled, and she can't remember the last time she lost her temper. She takes her husband's offbeat behavior perfectly in stride!

2. She probably is a very scholarly person who wouldn't dream of turning on the television set unless it's to watch the Public Broadcasting System. (Lucky her! She doesn't have to listen to her husband screaming his way through all those car commercials.) Really, she probably prefers the theater, and Shakespeare in particular.

3. She's likely to be rather introverted. She has a few close friends but feels out of place in a crowd and hates to be conspicuous.

Well, what I'm saying, of course, is that Mr. Flamboyant Last Born, the used-car salesman, is probably married to a prim and proper Firstborn. What's more, if that is indeed the case, they are probably very happy together!

It's certainly not my intention here to poke fun at the used-car salesman. This gentleman is using his natural tendencies to the greatest effect and is undoubtedly doing very well, thank you, selling those cars. It takes a special man to do the things he does—and he knows exactly what he's doing. He owes a great deal of his success to his wild and crazy commercials, and he owes another big portion to his steady-as-Gibraltar wife.

I've said before that I don't think everyone has to be married to be fulfilled in life. I don't believe that marriage is the be-all and end-all of human existence. Of course, because my own marriage is so terrific I tend to feel a little bit sorry for people who choose to remain single. But my greatest sympathy is reserved for those bachelors and bachelorettes who also happen to be Last Borns.

Dean Martin sang, "Everybody loves somebody sometime," and I know that's true, but it's especially true of Last Borns. Oh, we may try to be self-sufficient, but we're really not built to make it on our own. The old saying is that behind every successful man there is a good woman. That may not be true in all cases, but I would be willing to wager that it's true in at least ninety-nine percent of those cases where the successful man is a Last Born. And what's true for the goose is true for the gander as well, and so I'd say that behind every successful Last-Born woman there's a good man.

I'm sure you know by now, unless you've skipped the rest of the book and turned right to this chapter, that the good mate standing behind a Last Born is bound to be a Firstborn or a Middle Born with strong Firstborn tendencies.

I have seen some successful marriages featuring two Last Borns, yes, but I have also seen some Last-Born marriages that could have given the writers of *Dallas* enough storylines to last for the next five seasons!

What Kind of Firstborn Should I Look For?

To say that the Last Born matches up well with the Firstborn is fine and dandy, but of course it goes much deeper than that. There are many types of Last Borns, just as there are many types of Firstborns. It is true that most Last Borns have certain characteristics in common—but there are important variations too. If you've forgotten what the general tendencies of the Last Born may be, go back and take another look at Chapter One. But in addition to these general characteristics there are several additional factors that enter into the makeup of the Last-Born personality. Consider the various types of Last Borns:

1. Youngest brother of boys
2. Youngest sister of boys
3. Youngest brother of girls
4. Youngest sister of girls
5. Youngest brother of boys and girls
6. Youngest sister of boys and girls

Let's try a game of mix and match now, and see if you've been paying attention to what I've been saying about the importance of mixed-birth-order marriages. The following is a list of the ideal mates for the various types of Last Borns I've listed above. See if you can match the varieties of Firstborns listed below with the varieties of Last Borns listed above:

1. Older brother of boys
2. Older brother of girls
3. Older sister of girls
4. Older sister of boys and girls
5. Oldest sister of boys
6. Oldest brother of boys and girls

You got them all right, didn't you? Well, in case you're not sure, here are the correct matches:

1. The youngest brother of boys with the oldest sister of boys
2. The youngest sister of boys with the oldest brother of girls
3. The youngest brother of girls with the oldest sister of girls

BEST ROMANTIC COMBINATIONS
FOR LAST BORNS

YOUNGEST BROTHER OF BOYS	OLDEST SISTER OF BOYS
YOUNGEST SISTER OF BOYS	OLDEST BROTHER OF GIRLS
YOUNGEST BROTHER OF GIRLS	OLDEST SISTER OF GIRLS
YOUNGEST SISTER OF GIRLS	OLDEST BROTHER OF GIRLS
YOUNGEST SISTER OF BOYS AND GIRLS	OLDEST BROTHER OF BOYS AND GIRLS
YOUNGEST BROTHER OF BOYS AND GIRLS	OLDEST SISTER OF BOYS AND GIRLS

4. The youngest sister of girls with the oldest brother of girls
5. The youngest sister of boys and girls with the oldest brother of boys and girls
6. The youngest brother of boys and girls with the oldest sister of boys and girls

Is it beginning to sound complicated? Perhaps a little hard to keep straight? Actually it's all very simple. Let's take a closer look at these Last Born-Firstborn matchups.

Youngest Brother of Boys and Oldest Sister of Boys

The primary reason why this match works so well is that the wife is going to know her husband so completely.

Since she grew up taking care of little brothers, she knows what boys are all about—and particularly younger boys, who are in need of occasional guidance and more-than-occasional tender loving care.

She may have put up with an awful lot at the hands of those little brothers of hers, but it is likely that she learned very early on how to handle them, and that means she can also handle the volatile and unpredictable personality of her Last-Born husband.

What is the youngest brother of boys like? Well, more than likely he:

—is stubborn and unyielding when he really wants something, but he changes his mind frequently about what he really wants;

—can be an excellent worker when he puts his mind to it, but can also procrastinate for days or weeks and then have to rush like crazy to get the job done in time;

—is likely to bring his problems on the job home with him but figures that's a fair trade-off, because he also takes his problems from home to work with him!

—takes and spends easily because money just doesn't matter that much to him. Because of this he won't always appreciate the generous gifts of others, but he'll also be able to give generously without thinking twice about it.

—is not really a leader of men, but people seem to like him. As far as he's concerned that's just great, because there's nothing more important than being liked.

—is probably going to be more of a playmate than he is a father when it comes to his children. He's likely to joke and laugh with them and take their side when Mom tries to discipline them. He's also likely to act this way when the time comes for the parent-teacher conference, and regard any of the teacher's complaints about his child's behavior as "picking on" the child.

Beyond all of this the youngest brother of boys may pretend to be a rebel, but that isn't his true nature at all.

He'll continuously make statements to the effect that he wants to be free of some constraints, but you can chalk most of it up to sound and fury signifying nothing.

He may tell his wife, for instance, that he hates his job, and that he's going to quit and find something else to do with his life. He feels tied down, fenced in, and so on. Meanwhile his wife is on edge, wondering if he's really going to march into his boss's office and quit. But he's not likely to do that. He may take a step or two toward freedom, but he'll always go running back to the safety of the fences.

In the worst cases he might even tease his wife in this way about the marriage:

"Boy, I'd give anything if I were single again. I had a great time back then. Yes, sir, I must have had rocks in my head to give all of that up."

The woman who is married to a Last Born who talks like that would do well to understand that it's merely his birth order talking, and that he really doesn't feel that way. And then she can give him a good rap on the knuckles and hope that he'll dispense with all the I-gotta-be-free nonsense!

Actually I'm only teasing about the last part—but if his I'm-a-rebel tendencies are strong enough, his mate may want to follow the procedure described above.

One of the primary reasons the male who is the youngest of brothers goes together so well with the female who has several younger brothers is because he wants and needs to be nurtured, and she wants and needs to nurture.

I'm not talking about anything here that borders on the psychotic. I'm not saying that this gentleman will go around calling his wife "mommy" and that she'll have to tell him to sit up straight and stop chewing with his mouth open. When the world gets him down, he will be especially prone to run to the shelter of his wife's loving arms—and there's certainly nothing wrong with that. He may be prone to forgetting doctor and dentist appointments and need someone to remind him of them. In fact, he may be resistant to visiting the doctor at all, and his wife may need to give him a good, hard push to get him to have regular checkups.

There's a lot of little boy in any man, but especially in the man who's always been the "little" brother.

Just remember that the key to understanding any youngest male is to focus on the mother-son relationship. Is it a good one? If it isn't, guess who's going to end up paying a heavy price because of it? That's right, any woman who takes him for her husband.

And, if the youngest male shows signs of being a mama's boy, then watch out, because any woman who marries him is going to have her work cut out for her as she tries to get him to "stand up and be a man."

Youngest Sister of Boys and Oldest Brother of Girls

This is another ideal match, and both of these people should feel very comfortable being married to each other.

What are some of the special characteristics of the Last Born who is the only girl in the family?

—First of all, she's likely to be a "good sport." Life is not always a bed of roses for the youngest boy in a family of boys, but it can be even worse for the girl in that position. For one thing, the boys don't know how to treat a girl, so they probably treat her like another boy. She's likely to be included in the roughest of their games, victimized by their practical jokes, and so on. They may tease her when she's young about the fact that she's a girl, and even though their attitude is going to change dramatically as the years go by, chances are that she will have developed a thicker-than-average skin, which allows her to "grin and bear" whatever disappointments may come her way.

—She is also likely to be very feminine—partly, perhaps, as a reaction against the attitude of her brothers and those people who have always considered her "one of the boys." She goes along with the old song from *Flower Drum Song*—"I Enjoy Being a Girl." Her femininity has always brought her special attention and undoubtedly always will. She enjoys looking pretty and sexy and doesn't mind at all having the spotlight aimed at her.

—She will tend to be loyal to her husband, even if he turns out to be somewhat less than worthy of that loyalty. She will tend to put up with a great deal more than she should put up with. For example, the Last Born who was the only girl in her family is much more likely to put up with a husband who is an alcoholic or who may be abusive. As I said earlier, she is likely to enjoy the attention that other men give her because of her femininity and beauty, but there is nothing in all of this that says she will be disloyal to her husband.

—She tends to get along better with men than she does women. That makes sense, since the ones who were closest to her when she was growing up were boys. On the job she'll be liked and respected by her male colleagues, but the usual attitude of the women will be to want to keep her at arm's length. Part of the problem where the other females are concerned is that this "little sister" is going to be naturally attractive to men, and like most Last Borns, she is going to enjoy the attention she gets. She appreciates being the "star" attraction, although she may not have any idea what she does to get all this attention. The other women around her, though, may see her as calculating and manipulative where men are concerned, and they may resent it.

—Politically and religiously she is likely to follow the lead of her father and mother. She is more than likely going to believe in God, view him as a loving father, and want to live in accordance with God's teaching. She will be loyal to her religion, just as she is loyal to her husband, just as she was always loyal to her brothers.

The reason she matches up so well with the Firstborn brother of sisters is that they are exact opposites in so many ways. For instance, he is going to be rather uncomfortable around men, while he understands and appreciates women. He is going to be the type of man who believes in chivalry, who admires women, and who, when he falls in love, really falls in love. He is not likely to mind his wife being in the spotlight and will be happy when his friends think he's made a pretty good catch!

He will also be able to be a good influence with regard to some of her more careless Last-Born traits. For instance, she may have the tendency to spend money compulsively, occasionally even foolishly, while her Firstborn husband is going to be much more financially responsible. Because she is loyal to him and wants to make him happy, she is very likely to curb her natural tendencies and learn to be more responsible herself.

One thing the Last-Born female with brothers can know about the Firstborn male with sisters is that he is not likely to be the type of man who will fall in love with a woman just because of her appearance. He's not likely to be one of those who don't know the difference between love and lust. If he has a healthy relationship with his sisters, he'll know that feminine beauty is much more than skin deep, and he'll act accordingly. He may be attracted to a woman because of her intelligence, her kindness, because she's sensitive. In other words it is the heart and character that attract him to a woman more than anything else. She can know that he didn't make a flip decision that "Well, this one's okay, so I guess I'll marry her."

Because he doesn't enter into a relationship lightly, he is likely to be as loyal to her as she is to him. He doesn't choose a wife with the same attitude one might use to buy a suit or a car: "If this one doesn't turn out to be quite what I wanted, I can always get another one."

Many of the women I counsel tell me the same thing about their husbands, and it goes something like this: "He loves me when he wants my body, but outside the bedroom he doesn't seem to care a thing about me."

That doesn't paint a flattering picture of men in general, and I really do think that men need to learn to do a better job of showing their love and appreciation to their wives. But if there is any man in particular who is likely to do that, it's the Firstborn male who is also the only boy in his family.

Even though this birth-order combination is a good match, it's not without specific problems that may arise.

For instance:

Phillip was the Firstborn in a family where the three other children were all girls. Leah was the Last Born in her family, the girl her parents had always wanted after four boys in a row.

Phillip's little sisters treated him like a king. If he was thirsty, one of them would run into the kitchen and get him a glass of water. If he wanted to watch the football game, they would gladly sacrifice the movie they had been wanting to watch, and so on. They idolized their brother, and while he didn't treat them badly, he certainly didn't mind letting them wait on him either. Naturally, when he and Leah were married, he figured she would continue to dote on him and do everything within her power to see that he was happy.

Boy, was he ever dreaming big dreams!

Because Leah, meanwhile, grew up as the special little princess of her family. And no wonder, because Mom and Dad had wanted a daughter for so long, and when they finally got one they pampered and spoiled her terribly. Her brothers might have been expected to resent their parents' special treatment of the "little princess" and do something to bring her back down to earth, but they didn't. Instead, perhaps because they wanted to earn their parents' approval, they also treated her like royalty. When she got married, she expected her husband to wait on her too.

Well, you can bet that their marriage almost didn't make it through the first year. There were numerous arguments, and they covered just about every aspect of married life. They disagreed over what they were going to eat for dinner, what TV show they were going to watch, and over whose parents they were going to visit when the next holiday rolled around.

Fortunately Phillip and Leah really did love each other. And it was another piece of good news for the marriage that they were both intelligent people who knew that the other partner wasn't entirely to blame for the difficult situation. Eventually they were able to work out a compromise.

At first they tried giving in to each other all the time, but it didn't work because each one knew the other's heart wasn't really in it.

When they were going out to a movie and Phillip said, "You go ahead and decide what we're going to see, because it doesn't really matter to me," Leah knew he was lying through his teeth, and that only made her angry.

"Look! I know there's something you really want to see. Why won't you tell me what it is?" Now, chances are the movie he wanted to see wouldn't have been the one she wanted to see, and his telling her about it didn't mean that she'd go along with him. And, of course, the reverse was true too. Phillip knew Leah too well to let her get away with lying to him about her desires.

Besides, it's hard to tell your wife you really wanted to see the new Dustin Hoffman movie when you've got your teeth clenched so hard, the words have a hard time getting past them.

What they did was decide that they would take turns making the "important" decisions, or at least the decisions that would have normally caused an argument between them.

If last week Leah had picked out the movie they were to see, then it was Phillip's turn to choose this week, and so on. Perhaps it sounds petty, but it was a way to make sure that they were both getting their way at least fifty percent of the time and that no one was getting stepped on.

After a while they began to dispense with the recordkeeping, and it became more and more natural for each to give in to the other's desires.

The key, here, as in all other problems that arise between married couples, was love, communication, and compromise. But the problems that existed between Phillip and Leah demonstrate those that can arise even in an "ideal" birth-order marriage.

Another problem that arose in a marriage between a Last-Born sister of boys and a Firstborn brother of girls had to do with travel.

Last-Born Sherry loved to travel, while Firstborn Greg was a stay-at-homer, who could hardly bear the thought of being on the road. Greg occasionally had to go on business trips, although not very often, and it's a good thing, too, because whenever one of his trips was pending, he'd almost develop an ulcer just thinking about it. He didn't know, really, if it was the prospect of traveling that made him uneasy, or the prospect of being away from his wife and children. But part of the problem was that traveling disrupted his comfortable routine, you see, and Greg was very set in his ways. I've said before that the Firstborn is very often a stabilizing influence on the Last Born, but in this case Sherry felt that he was more like an anchor. He was tying her down, and she wanted to get out and see the world. And unfortunately his business trips were usually arranged in such a way that he went with several other men from the office—and there was no room for wives.

Sherry had occasion to go on one or two trips for her company and asked Greg to come along, but he wouldn't. The couple would occasionally travel to a city some 125 miles away from where they lived and spend a night or two in a motel. This was a great adventure to Greg, but Sherry didn't think it counted much toward her desire to "see the world."

Sherry teased Greg about his lack of adventure and called him an old fuddy-duddy—or something like that—but it didn't do any good. Actually, though, Greg didn't suspect the true extent of Sherry's anger over his refusal to go with her, or her boredom.

Again, the biggest key to the relationship was communication.

Greg didn't have a phobia about travel. There was no reason he couldn't take his wife on a trip once in a while. Sherry had to go beyond teasing and tell her husband how she really felt. She had to express her anger and resentment, as calmly but as truthfully as possible, and ask her husband to work at making some changes in his life-style.

I truthfully didn't see a thing wrong with Sherry's attitude in this whole matter. Had she wanted to be going somewhere every weekend, I think Greg would have been right to resist. She would have to be considerate of his feelings as a routine-oriented First-born. But one or two trips a year, as long as they could afford it, certainly wasn't too much to ask—especially when Greg was aware that his wife's birth order had instilled in her an adventurous nature. She loved seeing new places and new people.

There were three options available to this couple.

1. Sherry could have changed her attitude and sat at home with

her husband week after week. That wouldn't have done much good, though, because she surely would have become more resentful, bored, and restless.

2. Sherry could have traveled without Greg, perhaps with another woman or a group of women friends. Although this option was much better than the first, it wasn't something I would recommend, either, because it was likely to encourage the two of them to grow apart. Admittedly husbands and wives need time apart from each other. There's no need to suffocate each other—and I think it's perfectly fine for husbands and wives to take separate trips every now and then. But to make it a continual habit invites trouble into the marriage. They say that absence makes the heart grow fonder, but they also say, "Out of sight, out of mind," and anyone who allows his mate to wander all over the continent while he stays at home is flirting with danger.

3. The third and best option was for them to compromise. To their one or two annual weekend trips Greg agreed that they would add one or two longer journeys each year—traveling a total of two weeks—and the rest of the time they would stay at home. It's true that Greg was making the biggest move, but he was not surrendering nearly as much as Sherry would have by giving up her desire to travel. Asking Greg to alter his routine for two weeks out of a year wasn't asking an awful lot.

I know this sounds like a legalistic approach to the problem. But having Greg commit to these two trips a year was much better than having him make a nebulous statement such as "I'll try to travel more." It also gave the couple something concrete to work with, so that Sherry wasn't able to demand four, five, and six trips a year.

Over the next few years the two of them grew more toward the center. Greg found that he didn't mind traveling as much as he'd always thought he would, especially if Sherry—and sometimes the kids too—was along with him. Sherry continued to enjoy travel, but she became more content to stay at home throughout the rest of the year.

This is what usually happens to people who learn how to compromise. They find that they really do enjoy the change and wish they had been willing to make it years before.

Have you ever tried to get a child to eat something he already knows he's not going to like?

"Come on, Sarah, just try it, I think you'll like it!"

"No!"

"Please, for me?"

"No!"

"If you try it, I'll give you a dime."

"Well . . . okay."

So you put a small taste of whatever it is into Sarah's mouth. She starts chewing with a disgusted look on her face—but the more she chews the more that expression changes. It's just as you thought—you figured she'd like it and she does. But will she admit that to you? Of course not!

"How'd you like it, Sarah, honey."

"It was awful. . . . Er . . . but can I have another bite?"

Too often those of us who are adults don't want to admit to anyone—even our mates—that they've caused us to have a change of heart, and that we actually like something we always thought we would detest. Husbands and wives who really do love each other need to be willing to compromise, to change, and to be willing to say, "I was wrong." This is true whether the marriage is one that is predestined by birth-order similarities to have a number of problems, or whether it's an ideal birth-order matchup. It doesn't matter who you are or when you were born, "happily-ever-after" doesn't come without working at it.

Youngest Brother of Girls with Oldest Sister of Girls

This Last Born is going to be the sort of person who brings out the maternal instinct in women, and the oldest sister in a group of girls is likely to have great maternal urges stirring within her being.

This young man has grown up with girls who have, more than likely, doted on him, cared for him, and generally treated him like one of their cuddly toys. This is the same sort of treatment he is going to look for in a wife, and the best place he'll find it is in the oldest sister of girls—although he is also likely to find it in the oldest sister who has only brothers.

The reason he does so well when matched up with the oldest sister of girls is that he is not likely to be as competitive—in a masculine sense—as men who grew up with brothers. Because of this, and because her upbringing did not bring her into day-to-day close contact with boys, the oldest sister of girls is going to understand and appreciate this particular birth order better than she would any other man.

This Last-Born male has many tendencies typical of all Last Borns. For instance he may change his plans repeatedly and be totally inconsistent, but at other times he may insist on seeing a job through to completion, even if it would be better for him to walk away from it for a while.

He also tends to put things off until the last minute and then have to rush to get things done. He tends to work well under pressure, or at least his co-workers think he does, but the truth is that the pressure is almost always artificial and that he brought it upon himself. He puts himself in a position where his back is against the wall, and then he is forced to perform or else. Sometimes it almost seems that he's incapable of performing unless he feels things closing in on him.

What are some of his other characteristics?

—He can lose himself in his work and let every other area of his life fall apart. For this reason he desperately needs an organized woman who will help him stay on top of things when his "one-track mind" has closed out all but one facet of his existence.

—He is not usually a terribly good father. Whether he wants to admit it or not, he may see his children as competition for his wife's favor and attention. This doesn't mean he's likely to be abusive to his children or treat them indifferently, but he is likely to let his wife be the one in charge when it comes to parenting. He may, in fact, be a very good companion to his children. But when it comes to practical matters, such as problems at school, or other crises that children all face, he may not be much good. That's another reason why it's a very good match for him to be paired with a Firstborn sister of girls, who usually has highly developed maternal instincts.

—When it comes to women, he is perfectly at ease. He knows the right words to say to win their approval and usually won't hesitate to say them, whether or not he means them. That's not to say that he's a ladies' man, or that he intentionally sets out to deceive anyone. It's important to him that other people—and especially women—are happy, and he knows how to say things that will make them happy. He's had plenty of practice with his sisters!

—If his flattering comments to other people seem to be shallow, don't be too hard on him. The truth is that he usually doesn't see very far below the surface when he's dealing with others. He is simply not very good at perceiving the true needs, desires, and motives of others. This is another part of his life where the Firstborn sister of girls is going to be able to complement him so well. She is usually able to size people up in a fairly accurate fashion. She's not cynical, but she's not gullible, either, and her abilities in this regard may keep her husband from making some major mistakes in business or other important areas of his life. Of course, he has to understand and appreciate his wife's perceptive nature, and he has to be willing to listen to what she has to say.

—It is also true that while he relates to women in general better than he does to men, he also relates better to men who are younger than he is. This is because they are less likely to be in direct competition with him, and he is uncomfortable competing with other males.

—When it comes to religion, he is likely to be indecisive and would prefer to keep one foot in the kingdom of God and the other foot in the world. It isn't that he doesn't take religion or the quest for the meaning of life seriously, it's just that he is inconsistent here, as he is in other areas of his life, and isn't always sure what he believes or why. He may go through periods of being totally immersed in religion, and then seem cold and indifferent at other times. Ultimately he is likely to return to the faith or beliefs of his parents and may rise to an office of honor within the church. He is likely to be an example of someone who has done quite well both in the world and in the church—especially if he has a Firstborn wife whom he can lean on and who will keep him pointed in the right direction when too many confusing issues are demanding his time and attention.

There are many, many pluses in a marriage of this type, although there can occasionally be problems even here. For instance, one couple, Adam and Lindsey, ran into problems because Adam came to feel that he was living in his wife's shadow. She was a sterling example of a Firstborn achiever and seemed to be perfect in almost everything she did—at least that was the way she seemed to Adam, whose own flaws were magnified when he compared himself to his wife.

People seemed to notice Lindsey, they always complimented her on her appearance, she always had clever things to say, and she never seemed to be taken by surprise. Whatever came along, she was ready for it. That's how organized she was.

The primary problem here, as you've probably guessed, was that Adam was feeling left out and ignored. Like most Last Borns he had a need to be in the spotlight, but it's hard to get anyone to notice you if you're a peasant who happens to be standing next to the queen. The situation wasn't about to destroy his life or his marriage, but Lindsey knew that even though Adam tried to be a good sport about it, he still needed more time in the spotlight.

It certainly wasn't Lindsey's fault that her own perfection seemed to bring out feelings of inferiority in her husband. And I wasn't going to ask her to purposefully mess things up once in a while. The solution was not to change Lindsey, but to improve Adam's outlook.

Here again, as in nearly all problems that may arise within a marriage, action on the part of both partners was necessary. Adam needed to learn to enjoy relinquishing the spotlight to his wife and allowing her to shine. Lindsey, though, was determined to do what she could to get attention for Adam—and she did it in simple but effective ways.

—When his birthday came, she gave him a surprise party, which he thoroughly enjoyed, and did her best to stay in the background throughout the evening.

—Adam liked to write amusing stories about the things that went on in the family, which Lindsey had always enjoyed. She encouraged him to submit some of his articles to the local newspaper, and when a few of them were published, that increased his stature within the couple's circle of friends.

—In social situations, when she sensed that her husband felt left out, she would purposefully direct the conversation to an area in which he was particularly articulate and at ease.

In these ways she was allowing her husband to enjoy his moments in the limelight—something that every human being needs, and especially the Last Born. Remember, too, what was said earlier, about Adam's birth order giving him the natural ability to bring out the inherent maternal instincts in a woman who was the oldest born of girls. Obviously he was bringing out all of those maternal and protective instincts in Lindsey. If he had been married to another Last Born who shared his desire to be the center of attention, the minor crisis might have escalated into an all-out war instead of being resolved so peacefully and so quickly.

Did I hear someone say, "How silly"? Are you thinking that Adam was a big boy and that he should have been responsible for his own happiness? Well, let me tell you right now that when two people really love each other, they are willing to support each other and sacrifice for each other. Every human being has weaknesses in his character. I imagine that even George Bush, the leader of the free world, occasionally acts like a child.

Unless you're willing to support your mate when he is weak and do your best to understand his shortcomings, you probably shouldn't get married at all!

For instance, Adam didn't want to be resentful of Lindsey's

being the center of attention, but as much as he tried to be happy about it, he couldn't help but be envious and wish that others would notice him more. So he did his best to change his attitude, she did her best to get him his day in the sun—and the two of them made it safely through this minicrisis.

Youngest Sister of Girls with Oldest Brother of Girls

By now it should be fairly apparent why a marriage of this type would work so well.

So, if you're a Last-Born female who has older sisters, go out and nab yourself a guy who was the Firstborn and who had only sisters.

Why?

Because among other things, the oldest brother is likely to be gentle and considerate toward women. If he has a good relationship with his sisters and his mother, then he's quite likely to have a good relationship with you as well. This man is going to cherish the love and respect of women above all else in life. That's because it was primarily the way his sisters looked up to him that gave him his importance and self-worth when he was a child—and as a grown man he still looks to women to support him in that way. He will want to protect and look out for the woman in his life and will need a partner who won't feel stifled or suffocated by this, but who will appreciate it instead.

When he meets a woman who is the Last-Born sister of girls, he's probably going to feel he's on the right track.

Thus it's true, too, that when this Last-Born girl finds a man who has been the oldest child and only boy in a family, she has found someone to give her the loving nurturing she needs.

Like other Last Borns this woman is going to be capricious and willful. She's likely to change her entire outlook on life at a moment's notice. She's spontaneous, easily bored with routine, and craves adventure.

Again, it should be easy to see by now why a solid Firstborn male is going to complement her so well.

She is a very good catch for the Firstborn male—if he can catch her at all. This lady is usually particularly attractive to men, but because she is so changeable and uncertain about what she wants, she may be seen as "fickle" or elusive. Before she is married, she is prone to wanting the man until she has him, and then boredom sets in and she needs another conquest. This is not to say that she is going to be unfaithful to the man she marries, but rather that she is not going to go into marriage easily. When she finally decides to commit her life to a man, it is going to be because she loves him completely—although it is possible for her to change her mind about this later on.

Part of her attractiveness to men, incidentally, is her submissive nature—or perhaps I should say her seemingly submissive nature, because it's not always the real thing. She's capable of getting what she wants from people—and particularly from men—by acting submissive to them. She's not being devious—it's just that a youngest child seldom gets her way by being overpowering, so she takes advantage of her "weakness" to get her way.

She may tell her husband, for example, that she wants to go wherever he does for their next holiday trip—and that she wouldn't dream of imposing her wishes on him. At the same time, she lets it be known in various ways how much she misses her parents, and how it really would mean a lot to her to see them. What will eventually happen is that her "stronger" husband will decide that they can spend the holidays with her parents.

It's been his decision, you see, and he feels good about that. He also feels good about the fact that he was able to do something to give his wife pleasure and thereby increase his stature in her eyes. Meanwhile his wife got what she really wanted all along.

Please understand that I am not suggesting that if this is your birth order you are going to be manipulative and sneaky, or that you are always going to resort to using your "feminine wiles." But you will use your "Last-Born wiles," and it will be so much a part of your nature that you'll do it without really thinking about what you're doing.

Let's take a very brief look at a few of the other characteristics of this birth order:

—On the job, she is not going to be a good leader or boss over others. She is capable of being a good worker, but the boss who will get the most out of her will probably be a male who tries to overlook her faults and who is too old to be a romantic interest.

—When it comes to children, she is likely to enjoy them and relate to them well on a friendly basis but would prefer that her husband take the lead when it comes to discipline and trouble-shooting. This is something the Firstborn male won't mind doing anyway, as he exercises his natural desires and abilities to be in charge.

—She can be quite creative but doesn't have enough patience to use those abilities to their fullest capacity. She's in too much of a hurry to spend the necessary hours on any one project, you see. But if she has a husband who can help her to slow down and put a bit more effort into things, she may be quite artistic.

—She may appreciate the finer things in life but won't be good at hanging on to them once she has them.

—When it comes to religion and philosophy, she is probably going to be all over the road.

All of these personality characteristics show clearly why she is going to match up so well with a Firstborn.

If she is not married to a Firstborn who has younger sisters, the second-best match is a Firstborn who has younger brothers; but, according to Walter Toman, "they may find they are missing something that they cannot quite name."[1] The truth is that there is not likely to be as much passion in this match. I am not speaking of sex here, because they may have a terrific time in the bedroom, but because he has had no sisters, he truly lacks the understanding of women that would be necessary to arouse her most feminine instincts and keep them aroused.

If this is your birth order, you may also be compatible with a

Middle Born, but the Middle Born in question should have at least one sister and have some strong Firstborn tendencies.

Your absolutely poorest matchup would be with the youngest brother of brothers. In this situation, not only because your Last-Born traits would be compounded by his, but also because neither one of you really know very much about the opposite sex—at least in a psychological sense—and so wouldn't be too likely to be understanding and supportive of each other.

Other Potential Matchups

When we were talking about potential marital matchups for the Last Born, we mentioned that the Last Born who has older brothers and sisters is going to match up well with the Firstborn who also has brothers and sisters.

In fact, a combination of this type is probably going to be the best of all.

If you're a Last-Born female who grew up with brothers and sisters, for instance, you're probably going to understand the psychological makeup of both males and females—and you'll get along well with both sexes.

Beyond this, all of the reasons why Last Borns and Firstborns match up so well apply to you.

To recap, let's take a look at some of the reasons why as a Last Born you are likely to be complemented so well by a Firstborn:

LAST BORN IS:	FIRSTBORN IS:
Capricious and changeable	Rock steady
Spontaneous and impulsive	Controlled and planned
Adventurous	Comfortable in a routine
Disorganized, even sloppy	Organized to a fault
Extroverted	Introverted
Easygoing	Perfectionistic and critical

Financially impulsive	Financially responsible
Quick to change his mind	Stubborn and resistant to change
The life of the party	The one who made sure the party went off without a hitch in the first place
An underachiever	An overachiever
Interested in being liked	Interested in being respected
An excellent team player	The leader of the team

I could go on for pages yet, showing the ways that Last Borns and Firstborns are likely to complement each other, but I'm sure that by now you have a fairly complete idea of the way things are likely to be.

If you're a Last Born, take an honest appraisal of yourself. Although you are not likely to be much of a list maker, get out a pen and a piece of paper and make a short list of your personality traits. List all of the things that make you feel good about yourself and your birth order, but also be honest and list some of the things you'd really like to change about yourself, but which seem a deeply ingrained part of your personality.

Once you've done that, make another list, this time of the traits you need to find in your lifetime partner. How will he best be able to complement you? And how best will you be able to complement him?

I am not trying to turn romance into a coldly calculated and clinical task. I believe in love and romance, but I also believe in comparison shopping.

Remember the old saying, Kissing doesn't last, but good cooking does. Well, it's also true that romance and sexual passion may cover up birth-order incompatibilities for a while—but not forever. The Last Born, as we've seen, tends to act impulsively in many areas of his life, but when it comes to romance, and especially to a romance that's going to lead to marriage, this is one time he'd better go against those natural tendencies, or he's likely to regret it later on.

Coming up next, a few more tips for the Last-Born detective.

10

Tips for the Last-Born Romantic Detective

Have you got your fingerprint kit, your Columbo trench coat, and your spyglass close at hand?

It's time for me to give the Last-Born romantic detective some guidelines about finding his lifetime partner. If you're not a Last Born, you might as well come along anyway, because you might gain an insight or two in the process. Along the way we're going to tell the Last Born:

—how to find someone who is not compatible with him, and why this is going to be one of the best possible moves he can make

—how to learn how to think like a Firstborn when it comes to romance, and why this is so important

—to be wary of a relationship with anyone who seems to want to encourage you in your vices

—how to give love a chance

—why the Supremes were right when they sang, "You can't hurry love"

—why Percy Sledge was right when he sang, "Take time to know her"

Let's start off by taking a look at the guidelines:

1. TRY TO FIND SOMEONE WHO IS NOT COMPATIBLE

Are you thinking that there's a typo here, and that what I really want to do is tell you how to find someone who is compatible with you? No, I mean it just the way I wrote it. If you as a Last Born truly want to be happy, you'd better go out and look for someone who isn't at all like you.

Take a close look at that person you're interested in.

Is she impeccably dressed while you prefer jeans and knit shirts to suits, can't wait to yank your tie off the minute you get home from work, and love weekends because you don't have to shave? Wonderful, that means you're incompatible. This relationship could go somewhere.

Does he turn the lights off in one room as he passes from that room to another, and does he go back and give the faucet another twist after you've already turned the water off—just to make sure it's not wasting water? Do you tend to leave all the lights on and not give a second thought as to whether you left the water running? Terrific! This sounds like a wonderful match to me.

You're bound to be every bit as happy as Todd Andrews and Shannon Newman are.

Before I tell you what Shannon Newman did, let me explain that she was and is a Last Born to the extreme—a fun-loving woman who never let anything stand in the way of her pursuit of a good time. Occasionally, if the situation warranted it, she was known to tell a fib now and again, although she assures me she has reformed and is doing her best to model her life after George Washington, who never told a lie. (Except maybe to a redcoat or two.)

Of course, you'd know she was a Last Born when I told you that she made two dates for the same night. Who else but a Last Born would do something like that?

Well, actually she made three dates for the same night. But she had the good sense to cancel one of them.

"I knew I wasn't all that interested in going out with Aaron, but I just couldn't make up my mind between Todd and David."

She kept thinking she was going to cancel one of the dates, but in a move that also can be fairly typical for a Last Born, she never got around to it. As it turned out, Todd was planning to pick her up for dinner at seven P.M., whereas David was planning to do the same thing at eight-thirty. She could call David and ask him to pick her up at nine-thirty. That way she'd at least be able to spend a couple of hours with Todd before asking him to take her home.

Before continuing with my story, let me tell you what sort of reaction I'm getting from people who are reading this. The Firstborns are thinking, *Nah, he's gotta be making this up. Nobody really does that.* The Last Borns are smiling and thinking that they've either done something similar or wouldn't mind doing so. And the Middle Borns aren't sure yet what they think. They're still thinking about the lack of pictures of themselves in the family photo album.

(The story is absolutely true, though the names may have been changed to protect the guilty party.)

As for Todd, he was a straitlaced no-nonsense overachieving Firstborn—with a master's degree in business administration from a top university, and his own business. Yet he was still in his twenties.

He had met Shannon in a nightclub, and they had shared a dance or two, but this was to be their first "real" date.

When the evening arrived, he picked her up at seven o'clock sharp, took her to his favorite restaurant, and they enjoyed getting to know each other over a leisurely dinner. Actually, though, it wasn't all that leisurely, because Shannon seemed to be somewhat preoccupied and impatient. Furthermore, she kept looking at her watch, and that didn't make Todd all that secure about how well the evening was going.

By eight forty-five they had finished dessert, and Todd asked her if she would like to go dancing, or perhaps take in a movie.

Think fast, Shannon.

"Oh, no. I'm sorry, but I really do have to get to bed early tonight, I have to get up early tomorrow." She offered some lame excuse that neither one of them heard. Either she was going to have to knit a dust bunny or attend her Franklin Pierce Fan Club meeting. It wasn't really anything so ridiculous, but it might as well have been to Todd, because he knew she was lying, and he felt humiliated and angry.

He didn't say much as he drove her home, and didn't ask to see her again, even though she assured him that she had had a wonderful time and hoped he would call her. She told him that after making the date she realized this probably wasn't going to be the best night, but she hadn't wanted to cancel the date out of fear that he wouldn't ask her again.

Then she went in the house to freshen up and get ready for her date with David—hoping that he didn't have reservations at a fancy restaurant.

Todd started to go home, but had driven only a half mile or so when he started thinking that maybe she really had been telling the truth. Besides, there couldn't be anything wrong with giving the girl the benefit of the doubt. He spent some time wrestling with the matter but finally decided to drive back to Shannon's neighborhood, park down the street from her house, and wait for a while. Naturally he saw David arriving for his date—so there could be no further doubt about what Shannon had really been up to.

She was certainly not the sort of woman a career-oriented First-born like himself ought to get involved with. He would just put her out of his mind and get on with his life. But that was much easier said than done, and although he was angered and hurt by what she had done, he was also intrigued by it. It made her seem more elusive, more mysterious, and it seemed to him that it would be more of an achievement to clip her wings.

He did some checking and came up with some other disturbing facts.

Shannon wasn't twenty-six, as she had told him, but thirty. Because he was twenty-eight, he figured she had told him she was twenty-six because she was afraid he wouldn't be interested in an "older" woman. That flattered him, but then of course it also bothered him because it was another sign of her deceitfulness.

He thought about that beautiful blond hair of hers and wondered what her hairdresser knew for sure.

Todd, you see, wouldn't lie about anything. He was scrupulously honest about everything, even including his income tax, and never tried to take more deductions than he had coming to him. He wouldn't lie about his age, he wouldn't put Grecian Formula on his hair to cover the gray—if he'd had any gray—and he certainly wouldn't make two dates on the same night and then lie about it!

He was so angry, he did the only thing he could think of. He called and asked her for another date. When she quickly agreed, he said, "And this time I want to be your date for the entire evening. Is that okay with you?"

She laughed it off. "Absolutely. Sorry about before."

"And by the way, how old did you say you are?"

"Er . . . don't you remember?"

"Twenty-six, wasn't it?"

"Yeah . . . twenty-six."

"Isn't it more like thirty?"

She laughed again. "Okay, thirty. Whatever you say!"

Good grief! The least one could expect was that she be embarrassed about the lies she'd told and the things she'd done.

Her laid-back attitude about everything drove Todd absolutely crazy. But when they were together, they had a wonderful time, and he found himself laughing more than he had in years.

And then, of course, she promised him that there would be no more fun and games, and no more lying. He couldn't tell if she had her fingers behind her back or not.

Less than a year later Shannon and Todd were married.

That was seven years and two children ago.

Today their personalities haven't changed all that much. Todd is still serious minded, goal oriented, and plans to retire by the time he's fifty. Shannon is fun loving, unhurried, and tends to take life as it comes.

You wouldn't have thought they were compatible nearly eight years ago. You still wouldn't think they were compatible today, just to consider their personalities.

So why are they so deliriously happy?

The truth is that they are a near-perfect example of a happily married couple whose personalities balance each other. Here is a couple who seem to be incompatible to the casual observer, but if you know about birth-order differences and the way they fit together, you can see why there are likely to be years of wedded bliss ahead for Todd and Shannon.

What do you, as a Last Born, look for in a potential mate?

That depends a great deal on your own personality, of course. However:

—If you'd lose your head if it weren't screwed on tight, you ought to get to know the person who believes that one of life's basic rules is a place for everything and everything in its place.

—If you've had six jobs in the last three years, and you meet someone who's been with the same company all that time, and is starting to work his way up the ladder, it might be worth giving him a second look.

—If you're an easygoing and somewhat sloppy Last Born who's out to dinner with someone in a fancy restaurant, and you notice that this person knows exactly what to do with every utensil and dish set in front of him, and that he just exudes confidence—you might want to try to get a little bit closer to this Firstborn.

—If you're an easy-spending Last Born, and your date talks at length about his investments, try not to get bored. This may be worth listening to.

—If your car is always a mess, with books, papers, and old McDonald's bags strewn everywhere, and his is absolutely immaculate, don't write him off as a "clean freak." He may be just what you need.

This is what I mean by looking for someone who is incompatible with you. Look for someone who is strong where you are weak— even if he's a little too strong. After all, if he's a really good guy except that he takes life too seriously, wouldn't it be great to get him to have a little fun in life?

2. TRY TO THINK LIKE A FIRSTBORN

Now, what was it Dr. Leman said in point number one? If I'm sloppy and the other person is . . . what was it? A brunet? Yeah, that's it. If I'm sloppy and the other person is a brunet, I ought to give him a second look.

I'm having a little fun here at the expense of the Last Borns in the audience, including myself. Remember that Last Borns aren't apt to read the instructions. They aren't apt to make lists. They tend to go by their feelings, without giving a great deal of thought to the consequences.

On Christmas Eve, all over America, Last-Born fathers are trying to put tricycles, bicycles, swing sets, and every other sort of complicated contraption together without giving the least bit of attention to the instructions. For some dads it's going to work fine because they have enough natural mechanical ability to carry them through. For other dads—myself included—what's supposed to be a tricycle is probably going to wind up looking like a Rube Goldberg invention.

And that's bad—but not nearly as bad as leaving love and romance entirely to chance. Don't put this book aside when you're finished with it and forget about everything you've read. It may go against your nature, but you really need to put these things into practice. That's what I mean by urging you to be more like a Firstborn. A Firstborn will take stock of himself, he'll make lists, he'll work at implementing the things he learns in books, et cetera. That's what I want you to do, even if you are a Last Born.

—Keep your eyes open and look for those signals that show you the other person's birth-order characteristics.

—Take a complete inventory of your personality's strengths and weaknesses, so you have a better idea of what to look for in a partner.

—Remind yourself that good things don't always happen when

you go with your feelings. Sometimes you have to follow your head instead of your heart in order to get to where you really want to go.

—Look at the problems in the potential mate's family. Specifically, what are the problems that his or her parents may have? Whatever you see there is going to affect your marriage.

—If you're interested in finding a lifetime partner, take stock of your relationships. Do any of the people you're seeing have marriage potential, or are you just wasting your time? I'm not suggesting that you dump old friends, but it very well may be time to broaden your horizons.

—If you're already married and would like things to be going better between you and your spouse, take stock of your birth-order characteristics—as well as your mate's—and see where you might work to make changes that will improve the situation.

3. BE WARY OF ANYONE WHO SEEMS TO ENCOURAGE YOUR VICES

When I was a kid, the Kiwanis Club of Williamsville, New York, sponsored a fishing contest behind a dam at a place called Island Park. Whoever caught the biggest calico bass would win a prize. The contest, of course, was divided into age groups.

I don't remember now what first prize was going to be, and it probably wasn't all that important anyway. The main thing for me was that I wanted some recognition, and winning first prize—or even second or third prize—was a sure way to get that recognition.

So . . . in order to get my moment in the sun, I stuffed several half-ounce sinkers down my fish's gullet. Unfortunately—or perhaps fortunately—my trick didn't work, and my fish, added weight and all, still didn't win a prize.

Later on, when I thought about what I had done, I realized it wasn't right, and I was actually glad that I didn't win a prize dishonestly.

But what if my parents had found out what I had done and praised me for my ingenuity?

Well, you can bet that I would have been encouraged to try the same stunt yet another time.

It is true that every birth order has particular vices and virtues. It's easy, especially if you're a Last Born who just wants to have a good time, to establish a relationship with someone who is quite content to be your partner in crime. But that's not going to work out in the long run, because you're only going to drag each other down and see your bad points multiplied.

—If you have a hard time sticking to a goal and your mate is the same way, how will you ever get anywhere?

—If you spend money carelessly and impulsively and your mate is the same way, someday you'll both be in financial trouble.

—If you're disorganized and a bit sloppy and your mate is, too, you may soon be buried under an avalanche of junk.

Remember that the operative word here is *if.* You may not be any of these things. But whatever your worst vices may be, you really don't want to get married to someone who has the same shortcomings.

4. GIVE LOVE A CHANCE

A particular problem for many Last Borns is the inability to stay on course. We always want to find the quick fix, or take the easy way out, but you just can't do that if you're looking to develop a serious relationship with someone of the opposite sex.

Love takes time and patience to develop.

Did she get on your nerves, so you think maybe it's time to look for somebody new? Well, it's impossible to have a real relationship with another human being without getting on each other's nerves once in a while.

Did he let you down and disappoint you, so you've decided the relationship is over? You'd do well to remember that nobody is perfect. It's likely that everyone you're really close to is going to disappoint you at one time or another, and you'll probably do the same to him.

Are you bored with her? If so, it's a good idea to ask yourself why. Could the fault be yours instead of hers? Are you looking for someone to be your partner or someone to entertain you?

Did you see somebody else who's even cuter than the guy you're seeing? Don't you know that you can't build a lasting relationship based on the color of someone's eyes or the straightness of his teeth?

If you are looking for love, then you have to give love time to develop. That may sound like an old platitude, but it's oh, so true.

I realize that every romantic relationship between a man and a woman isn't going to be the real thing. Some relationships are going to dissolve, and the principals will wind up going their separate ways. The problem for the Last Born, though, is that his impatience tends to doom relationships that really might otherwise develop into something pretty special.

The Last Born needs to remember that there are no perfect relationships or perfect people, and if you spend your life searching for someone who is perfection—and to a Last Born that's probably going to mean fun and sunshine all the time—then you're probably going to wind up disappointed and lonely.

5. THE SUPREMES WERE RIGHT WHEN THEY SANG "YOU CAN'T HURRY LOVE"

"Now, wait a minute, Leman! Are you trying to have it both ways here? First of all you say that Last Borns need to stay with a relationship long enough to allow it to develop. Now you're saying that the Last Born attempts to rush into a relationship. Which is it?"

Actually, this is another variation of the same problem.

The impulsive, live-for-today Last Born may flit from relationship to relationship because of his impatience, or for the very same reason he may want to rush into a commitment before it's time to make a commitment.

Unless the Last Born spends the time necessary to be sure he knows exactly what he's doing, he's likely to find himself in a mess. That's what Trudi did.

She was an A-minus student in high school who could have gone to a good college. She loved drama and wanted to do some acting in college. If she couldn't make it as an actress, she figured she'd like to come back to her hometown and teach drama in the high school there.

But then Jack swept her off her feet. He was tall, good looking, athletic, and, most important of all, had a terrific sense of humor. To spend a day with him was like spending a day in an amusement park—one exciting moment after another.

She decided to marry him. He worked as a messenger for a local company and didn't make very much money, but she figured things would work out. Her parents said no, but she told them there was nothing they could do because she was eighteen. Her parents asked her to think of the future, but she was in love and couldn't wait. He was all she saw, and he was all she wanted.

Four days after her high school graduation, they were married and Trudi went to work in a grocery store as a cashier.

The rest of the story is sad history—the sort of thing Tracy Chapman would sing a song about.

Jack drifted from job to job, never making much more than a minimum wage. His sense of humor began to grate on Trudi's nerves. He laughed about things that weren't that funny anymore. Six years later Trudi was still working as a cashier. She resented having given up her dream of spending her life working in dramatics. What's more, she realized she didn't love Jack and probably never really had. She hadn't known the difference between love and infatuation and hadn't given the relationship time to show the difference. After all, infatuation will dissolve over time, whereas love will grow. Poor Trudi was trapped. She was a strongly religious woman whose beliefs wouldn't allow her to divorce her husband, and besides, there was a child involved, so all she could do was try to pick up the pieces of her life and her marriage—and make improvements wherever she could.

6. PERCY SLEDGE WAS RIGHT WHEN HE
SANG ''TAKE TIME TO KNOW HER'' (OR
DON'T MESS YOURSELF UP TO SHOW
YOUR MOM AND DAD UP)

Yes, I admit this sounds an awful lot like, "You Can't Hurry Love," but there is a difference here—and besides, it gives me a chance to talk about two of my favorite rock 'n' roll oldies!

Have you ever heard Percy Sledge's song? It was one of the great soul classics of the sixties—it ought to be on everyone's hit parade—or at least on every Last Born's hit parade.

You see, in this song, Percy Sledge's mom keeps telling him that he's making a big mistake by marrying this woman. But Percy won't listen to her.

Now, the song doesn't say so, but my own impression is that Percy was a Last Born who had always been put down and told what to do, and he just wasn't going to take it anymore. When Mom said, "Please don't marry her until you know her better," that made him resolve to get married the very next week. He thought to himself, *I'm tired of other people trying to run my life. I'm going to marry her and we'll be deliriously happy together.* Well . . . did he ever live to regret that bit of impulsive behavior!

Let's go back to dear Trudi. She didn't really know Jack all that well when she married him, but she rushed into marriage anyway because she wanted to show everybody that she was smarter than they thought she was.

Her parents were saying, "Don't do it!"

Her friends were saying, "Don't do it!"

Her advisers at school were saying, "Don't do it!"

And so Trudi said, "I'm going to do it!"

The Last Born often feels that other people have put him down and told him what to do. They've doubted his competence, maybe even made fun of him, and let him know that he could never, ever hope to be as good as his older brothers and sisters.

So inside he's thinking, *Just wait! I'll show them!*

There is nothing the least bit wrong with that attitude. It can be good, especially when it causes the baby of the family to do everything within his power to rise to greater heights. But it can also be bad if it causes him to go against what other people are telling him just so he can prove that they're wrong and he's right.

Looking back, Trudi has to admit that was part of her attitude regarding her plans to marry Jack, and it got her into all kinds of trouble.

What I'm saying here is that you are not marrying for anyone but yourself. If you're marrying to show someone else up, or to prove that you're capable of getting a beautiful woman, or for any other reason except that you know and love the person you're going to marry, then you're marrying for the wrong reason and you're probably going to wind up as Trudi did.

Please, take time to know her, or him.

Last Born, it may be true that people don't show you a lot of respect because of your being the baby of the family. To have an attitude of "I'll show them" is terrific. But don't be in such a hurry to show them that you rush into something that is going to hurt you instead of help you.

Coming up next, we'll take a brief look at what to expect from a Last Born in the various "departments" of marriage.

The Last Born within a Marriage

Just as we've done earlier for Firstborns and Middle Borns, let's take a look at how the Last Born can be expected to "perform" within the various departments of a marital relationship:

1. AT WORK

We've already said that the Last Born is going to be a very good member of the sales force. He's likely to have the gift of gab, and this will not only serve him well where the customers are concerned, but with his bosses as well. They are probably going to like him—perhaps to the point where they will overlook some minor flaws in his record or performance.

The Last Born is not likely to be the big boss. If he gains that position, it will be because he knows this is the place to make some money to enable him to live the kind of life he wants to live, and not because he enjoys power or wants to be in a position of leadership.

If the Last Born is working for someone who is a strong leader and who has the ability to motivate people, he may be one of the best and most productive workers in the entire company. He doesn't want someone leaning over his shoulder all the time, but neither should he be left completely on his own. If the former happens he's likely to rebel and waste as much time as possible. If the latter is the case, he might decide that having a good time is more important than getting the job done on time.

If you're married to a Last Born, there are two special tendencies to watch out for where your mate's job is concerned. The first is a tendency to wait until a deadline is on top of him before he really gets busy on a project. He seems to perform better when the heat is on, but it isn't necessary for him always to get himself in difficult situations. He's going to need a gentle push now and then.

The second problem that arises is a tendency to want to make changes, whether those changes are warranted or not. She may come home and say she hates her job and wants to quit. You, as her mate, have to help her sort out whether those feelings are truly justified and ought to be acted upon, or whether it's just her Last-Born tendencies coming to the surface.

One other thing I have to say about the Last Born and his performance on the job is that you should never, ever write him off. Many Last Borns are late bloomers. They've lived in the shadow of others for most of their lives and aren't really sure what they can do on their own. For this reason they may be a bit tentative and uncertain at first, but once they begin to gain confidence and ability, they can soar to great heights.

2. DURING HIS LEISURE TIME

Fun, fun, and more fun!

The Last Born generally loves adventure. He'll want to travel, see new places, and meet new people.

He may be a joiner when it comes to social organizations, but it's probably going to be because he wants to have a fun time with fun people, and not because he's looking for prestige or extracurricular activities with which to beef up his resumé.

The Last Born is restless, so that means he's always looking for something new. He may become bored with the old activities, just when his mate is beginning to really enjoy them.

He may enjoy sitting at home in front of the fireplace with a marshmallow on a stick every once in a while. But not often, because he wants to make the most of his leisure time, and that means cram every minute full of something exciting to do.

If you're going to marry a Last Born, you'd better have your traveling shoes and your sense of adventure in good shape. Chances are good that you'll need both of them.

3. DEALING WITH FINANCES

If you take a survey of investment counselors and stockbrokers, you probably won't find very many Last Borns. Some, to be sure, but not very many.

The Last Born is quite capable of handling his money wisely. But he's even more apt to spend impulsively, to think that buy now, pay later was one of the best inventions to ever come along, and to be somewhat careless in the managing of his financial affairs. This is especially true if he has always had the (mis)fortune of having parents and siblings who treated him as the baby, and so never had to think twice about bailing him out of financial difficulty.

Another reason he may have difficulty handling money is that material possessions just aren't that important to him. Money is the means to get what you want out of life, and that's all.

If you are dating a Last Born who is not financially responsible, that might seem like a good trait at first. For instance, he may be extremely generous with his money and love to spend it on you. But stop and ask yourself if he can really afford it. His generosity, which seems like such a good trait now, may not seem so terrific once you're married to him and trying to manage a household budget.

If you are contemplating marriage to a Last Born, and he seems to be on top of things financially, don't think, *Well, I know he's a Last Born, so he's going to blow it sooner or later.* If he has typical Last-Born tendencies with regard to his handling of money, those should be obvious right from the beginning.

4. IN HIS SOCIAL RELATIONSHIPS

We Last Borns struggle with self-centeredness. At the same time we are people-oriented individuals. We love to be with people, and they usually love to be with us, so our selfish nature is tempered by our desire to have other people like us.

Last Borns aren't likely to have as many friends as outgoing Middle Borns, but we will have a large number of acquaintances. The Last Born may not be your best friend, but he's still on the list of people you want to invite to your party.

As I've said before, the Last Born isn't always the most perceptive person when it comes to knowing what other people are thinking, desiring, or what their motives are. He generally doesn't get that deep into people's psyches. It's not necessarily because he's shallow—it's just that he tends to take people at face value.

Flip Wilson's alter ego, Geraldine, used to say, "What you see is what you get," and that's pretty much true with Last Borns.

Part of the reason for this is that the Last Born wants to be independent, even if he's not. Mom and Dad were probably always ready to ride to his rescue and may have done so dozens of times —but he doesn't like that and his I'll-show-'em attitude manifests itself in a desire to be totally self-sufficient. You see, he needs other people, but he doesn't want to get close enough to them, because that might mean that he'll need them too much.

If you're married to or contemplating marriage to a Last Born, you will probably need to work with him, to coax him out into the deep waters of "sharing."

5. IN THE BEDROOM

First of all, Last Borns are affectionate by nature. They like to touch, hug, and kiss. And this affectionate behavior carries over into the bedroom.

Because they were the babies in their families, they were probably held and kissed more than the other children. Not only did Mom and Dad hold and hug them, but so did their older siblings —and chances are good that the babies didn't mind it at all.

The person who reaches out and touches you on the arm when she is talking to you is likely to be a baby. I'm not saying that touching someone is a sexual act—it's not at all. But my point is that babies don't hesitate to make physical contact with other people.

Another thing about babies that we've said many times before is that they are fun loving and adventurous. Put those two qualities together with their affectionate nature, and you'll come to the correct conclusion that the sexual aspect of marriage is of the utmost appeal to the Last Born.

Last Borns who have siblings of the opposite sex are likely to be more at ease with their identities as sexual beings, but I wouldn't bet against any Last Born being outperformed in the bedroom.

One particular problem, though, is that the Last Born may separate what goes on in the bedroom from the other parts of his existence. He may need to learn that if he expects his mate to respond to him sexually, he had better be more attentive to her needs the rest of the time—helping with the housework, learning to pick up after himself, listening to her when she needs someone to talk to, and so on.

6 . IN PARENTING

If you're looking for a mate who will be a strong disciplinarian and make those kids toe the line, then you're not looking for a Last Born.

If, on the other hand, you're looking for someone who's going to be a real pal to the kids, who'll get down on the floor with them and wrestle, the Last Born may be exactly what you're in the market for.

Remember, now, that every parent is going to relate most of all to the child who occupies his same birth position—so it's likely that your Last-Born spouse and your Last-Born child are going to be quite a team, especially if they are the same sex. For your own peace of mind you might want to keep those two separated! Two Last Borns can be quite a handful!

Seriously, the Last Born may be more than a little intimidated by the responsibilities of raising children and might look for ways to abdicate the "parental throne"—but don't let that happen. If you are married to a Last Born, or contemplating marriage to a Last Born, the two of you need to sit down and draw up some very specific rules regarding the rearing and disciplining of children. And then promise each other that you're going to stick to those rules. It will save a lot of wear and tear on your marriage, and on the children too.

7 . WHEN IT COMES TO STRESS

What's that? The Last Born get stressed out? I didn't know that having fun could be so hard on a person.

Well, the truth is that the Last Born is not as likely to get stressed out as the perfectionistic and overachieving First Born. But it does happen, and when it does the First Born is much more likely to seek help in dealing with it. The Last Born will probably deny that he has a problem and pretend to laugh it off when he's crying inside. If you perceive that your Last-Born friend or lover is stressed out, you will need to be extra understanding and patient, and still more patient in getting him to deal with the problem.

The most common reason Last Borns get stressed out is that all their fast living catches up with them. They spend themselves into a financial hole, and then when the bill collectors begin harassing them, they feel the weight of the world. They make snap decisions that aren't in their best interests and then have to face the stressful consequences.

The Last Born who has a mate who sees to it that his actions are responsible is not likely to have a serious problem with stress. And that's where you come in.

8. IN RELIGION AND PHILOSOPHY

For all of his outward adventure and rebellion the Last Born is likely to remain true to the religious beliefs of his parents.

Well, perhaps "remain" true isn't accurate. He may experiment with many different belief systems during his younger days, but sooner or later he will return to the faith of his youth.

He may not know why. It's not that he's studied everything else and come to the conclusion that his parents knew the truth after all. It's more likely that he "comes home" simply because he has decided that it is as good as anything else he has found, and also because it provides him with security in that it brings him back to his roots.

When it comes to religion and philosophy, the Last Born is not likely to be a deep thinker. It isn't that he isn't capable, but just that delving into the deepest secrets of the universe doesn't sound like a great way to spend an evening. He may become a minister or a church official, but even here his gift is going to be relating to his people and bringing them comfort and joy—rather than ferreting out great truths for them.

He'll be completely satisfied to leave the thinking of great philosophical thoughts to someone else. As for him, he'd just as soon watch *Monday Night Football!*

He will be going along with his natural tendencies if he doesn't worry overly much about whether he's living his life in accordance with religious teachings. He may think he can twist the rules here and "get away with murder," just as he's done in other areas of his life.

PART FIVE

. . . And the Greatest Is Love

11

Some Final Thoughts about Love

I was in Alberta, Canada, talking to two thousand high-school boys on the topic of sex and love.

I'd been asked to speak to some tough audiences before, but this one looked like it was going to be brutal. I knew the "sex" part of the topic would grab their attention, but I also knew they'd turn me off right away if I didn't hook them with what I had to say.

Most adult audiences are easy. They'll listen to you even if they don't care too much for what you're saying. But teenagers? The average attention span is something like 9.1 seconds and you can lose them in a hurry. And if you've lost them, they don't mind at all letting you know that they can't wait for you to get off the stage.

Behind me on the platform were several of the most important members of the school board—dignified, impeccably dressed, and obviously refined people. The young man who introduced me, a clean-cut seventeen-year-old, was student-body president.

As I looked out over the audience, the first words out of my mouth were "What do we call penises in our society today?"

The sea of faces before me was absolutely still. Had they heard what they thought they heard?

I was quite sure, at the same time, that I felt the heat rising on the stage behind me. Any moment I expected to hear a loud thump as the principal fainted.

But I persisted anyway.

"You heard me," I said. "What do we call penises? Okay . . . what did Mom call it?"

A brave young man raised his hand. I pointed at him and he yelled out one of the more common names.

"Very good!" I turned to the chalkboard behind me and wrote the name in large letters. "What else?"

Someone shouted out another name, and this time, too, I wrote it on the board behind me. By now pandemonium had broken loose. The boys were getting into the spirit of things, exchanging high fives and slapping each other on the back as they called out the most common locker-room names for the penis.

Once we had a good list on the chalkboard I asked the next question.

"Now . . . what about the female genitalia!"

I felt for a moment as if I were E. F. Hutton, because when I spoke, all conversation and laughing stopped, and everyone was listening to me.

"What's the matter?" I said.

No one responded.

"Are you going to be like the guy in Denver who told me, 'I'll tell you, but I won't tell you here.' What do you suppose he meant by that? Could it be that those names are dirty and vulgar? Could it be that they cheapen and demean the beauty of sexual love?"

I knew now that I had them and I could take them wherever I wanted to go.

Looking out over the audience I said, "I would guess that most of you are somewhere around fifteen or sixteen years old. But for just a moment let's imagine that it's ten years into the future. You're married . . . it's the middle of the night, and you're in bed with your wife."

This news was greeted with whistles and the sound of stomping feet from the peanut gallery.

"Aw, come on guys. You're both sleeping!"

"Boooooo!"

"And all of a sudden your wife pokes you in the ribs and wakes you up. You look over at the clock and notice it's three A.M. All you want to do is sleep.

"But then she pokes you again, a little harder this time. And she says, 'Honey, something's wrong. I'm sick!' "

This news is greeted with nothing but silence from my audience, but all eyes are upon me, and I can tell they're paying attention, so I go on.

"Now, you have to be up in a few hours to get ready for work, but you shake yourself awake because you know the woman you love needs you.

"You say, 'What is it, hon? What's wrong?' Well, she tells you that the room is spinning and she feels like she's going to throw up. She needs to get into the bathroom, but she doesn't think she can make it without your help."

I could tell that my young audience was taking all of this quite seriously, because the concern was showing on some of their faces.

I went on, "So you hop out of bed and run around to the other side so you can help her. On the way you stub your toe in the dark. It really hurts, but you don't have much time to think about it, because your wife is moaning and groaning, and you know if you don't hurry, it's going to be too late. You take her by the hand and help her sit up—then you pull her to her feet."

I began to walk across the stage, acting as if someone were leaning against me.

" 'Come on, hon,' " I said to the imaginary person, in my most soothing tones, " 'you're going to be all right.' "

"But you know what?" There was no response to my question, but I knew they were thinking the worst. And they were right.

"You're too late. You're about six steps away from the bath-room door when it happens. Your wife told you she thought she was going to throw up and she wasn't kidding. There it goes, all over the carpet."

"Oooooh, gross!"

"And, gentlemen, guess who gets to clean it all up?"

"Oh, no!" someone yelled, "Not me!" But his voice was not joined by the others.

"Oh, yes, you will. And you know why? Because you love her. And you know what else? When you're down on your knees, scrubbing that carpet, that's when you're showing what love is. In that moment you're coming closer to the reality of love than all the sexy movies you've seen, the filthy jokes you tell each other, and all the romantic cards you send to your girlfriends on Valentine's Day."

From that point they were eating out of my hand as I went on to tell them in more detail what love between the sexes is—and what it isn't.

I've done quite a bit of talking in this book about the importance of finding your most compatible partner, but as important as that is, it's just as important to remember that any successful marriage takes work and plenty of it.

Leman's Recipe for a Successful Marriage

Start out with a heaping portion of love.

Add an equal measure of putting your spouse first and mix together.

Sprinkle liberally with patience, kindness, understanding, and gentleness.

Mix in plenty of time spent together, but be sure to allow your spouse enough time and space of his own so that he is not "smothered."

Finally, check carefully to see that you have left the lines of communication open.

Don't worry about baking, because there's going to be plenty of "heat" in any marriage.

Love's Better than Romance

Some people make the mistake of thinking that romance is synonymous with love. It isn't. This is a close cousin to thinking that a successful marriage must be perfect in every way, and it's even more dangerous.

Don't be fooled into thinking that love consists of candlelight dinners, greeting cards with sentimental verses in them, or even romantic phone calls during the middle of the day. All of these things are nice, and I advise husbands and wives to do as much as they can to keep romance in their marriage—but we should never confuse these outward displays of affection with true love.

People who confuse love and romance often wind up in divorce court because they are susceptible to the dangers of romantic thinking. They may not know much about love, but they enjoy the feeling of being "in love." They go around with moonbeams in their eyes and stardust in their hair, and they're fair game for anyone who knows how to speak the language of romance.

I admit that "being in love" feels wonderful . . . going around with a natural high, feeling lightheaded all the time, thinking that this old world is a marvelous place. But there is a whole world of difference between having those feelings and loving someone. Yes, when you fall in love with someone, you will experience all of those feelings—but those feelings can also come about because you are infatuated, or because of the excitement of establishing a new romantic relationship.

I believe that love takes time. I believe there is such a thing as infatuation at first sight, but not love at first sight.

Another mistaken belief some people have is that when you fall in love it's something over which you have no control. You're just swept along like some poor guy riding a barrel down the Niagara

River toward the falls. You know you're going to be in for one whale of a ride, but there's nothing you can do to stop it!

Who decides whether to fall in love? You do. Who decides who to fall in love with? Again, you do. You may be attracted to someone. You may decide that you like someone and want to be with him or her. It may be a painful decision for you to decide that this person isn't right for you and you can't let yourself "fall in love," but you can do it.

In my private practice, I have counseled many people who have become involved in extramarital affairs. And even though some of the "experts" will tell you that an affair can actually strengthen a marriage, I've never come across a case in which an affair left a marriage stronger or made the party involved any happier. An affair causes pain, guilt, and mistrust, and although a marriage can survive an affair, it takes a while for it to get back to the way it was before one of the partners broke the wedding vows.

Why, then, do people become involved in affairs? I've heard a number of different excuses. Men tell me their wives are cold and unresponsive, while women say their husbands don't talk to them or treat them with tenderness. But as often as I hear these "traditional" reasons for becoming involved in an affair, I hear this one: "I just couldn't help myself."

Or "You know, Dr. Leman, I don't really know how it happened. We were just good friends, and the next thing I knew we were in bed together."

Now, that's a strange one, isn't it? It's like two good buddies— one who happens to be male while the other is female—are out for a perfectly platonic lunch together. But some bad guy slips something in their iced tea, or conks them on the head, and the next thing they know, they're waking up in a bed in some second-rate motel.

To that sort of talk I can only say, "Oh, come on, now! You mean to tell me you didn't see that a bedroom scene was obviously going to be a part of the next act?"

In a situation like this I believe that both partners knew exactly where they were headed, but neither wanted to admit it, because that would have "cheapened" things. It goes much easier on your conscience if you can convince yourself that it happened before you knew what hit you.

But my point is that even though two people may be attracted to each other, they don't have to give in to that attraction. You can either give in to it, or you can fight it. And if you have trouble fighting it, but it's not in your best interest to give in, then find a way to avoid the other person, and stay away from compromising situations.

This advice holds true for those who are married and who find themselves tempted to become involved in an affair, and for those who are looking for a marriage partner. You do not have to allow yourself to become involved with someone who is not good for you.

There are several questions that anyone who is getting serious in a romantic relationship ought to ask himself.

They are:

1. IS THIS PERSON GOOD FOR ME?

There are several other questions that come under the umbrella of this one. In other words, is he really helping me to be everything I can be? Does he seem to care about me and want what's best for me? How does he treat me?

2. WHY AM I ATTRACTED TO THIS PERSON?

You may be attracted to a member of the opposite sex for a variety of reasons. It could be his personality or her sense of humor. Perhaps he's the most intelligent person you've ever met, or you're impressed by her gentle attitude. But then again, it could be that you like his smile, his perfect teeth, or his muscular body. And a man, if he is being honest, may have to admit that he is attracted to a woman because she has a beautiful face, soft silky hair, or a nice pair of legs. If you stop to think about what attracts you to someone, and have to admit that you just like the way he or she looks, then you'd better think about walking away from the relationship. A mutual physical attraction is no basis for anything but the shallowest of relationships, and it is definitely nothing on which to build a lasting marriage.

3. WHY IS HE ATTRACTED TO ME?

So this person is in love with you. Has he ever told you why he loves you? If he hasn't, go ahead and ask him. It's important to find out what the other person sees in you that makes him love you. And then ask yourself whether you really love this person, or if you think you do simply because he loves you. In other words, it's flattering to have someone tell you that he or she is in love with you. That in itself is enough to set some people's hearts fluttering. It may sound cruel, but you are under no obligation to love someone back just because he says he's in love with you.

4. WHAT DO I HOPE TO GET FROM THIS RELATIONSHIP?

Some people enter into a relationship because of what the other person can do for them. A man may want to be seen with a beautiful woman because he'll be the envy of other men who see them. He may actually think the woman is shallow or boring. But his friends will nudge him in the ribs and say, "How in the world did you catch a beauty like her?" and he enjoys their jealousy. (And, of course, a woman may be seeing a man for the same reason.) A woman may be dating a man because he has plenty of money to spend on her, and she likes the things he can give her. There are all sorts of reasons people get involved in a romantic relationship, and some of them make as much sense as trying to make a living selling snowshoes in my hometown of Tucson. For any relationship to succeed, both parties must make an honest and complete assessment of what they are really looking for in the relationship.

I'm not attempting to tell you how to know if you're in love. That's an age-old question that's been asked by poets and songwriters for centuries. Neither am I attempting to dissect the emotion of love and explain it to you in clinical terms. I may not be the world's most romantic person, but neither am I the sort who would take love into the laboratory and attempt to dissect it.

You may look the relationship up one side and down the other and still not know if it's love. You'll know it's something good, and that you're enjoying it, but just what it is you're not sure. And that's okay. But though you may not know if you're in love, there are other times when you know that you're *not* in love. And if, when you look at a romantic relationship, you know for certain that you're not really in love but that you're in it for some other reason, it's time to get out—no matter what that other reason may be.

5. IS THIS RELATIONSHIP BUILDING MY SELF-WORTH, BRINGING ME JOY, AND ENCOURAGING MY DEVELOPMENT AS A PERSON?

A few years back there was a hit song by a group called Nazareth, called "Love Hurts."

This song was all over the radio for a while, and I can still remember the lead singer wailing about how terrible love is. The only lyric I can remember is "Love hurts, love hurts," over and over.

A few years later there was another group, The J. Geils Band, which performed a song called "Love Stinks." Now, there's a sentimental song for you.

My question is, do you agree with those songs? Does love hurt? Does it stink? If so, the situation you're in isn't good for you, and it's time to get out quickly.

I'm not suggesting that there aren't times when love hurts. Lovers have misunderstandings, let each other down, and hurt each other. But if you're involved in a relationship which is seventy-five percent pain and twenty-five percent good times, then the relationship isn't good for you, and it really is that simple. I would never tell you to get involved in a relationship for what you can get out of it—but if someone really loves you he will support and encourage you, and seek to lift you up.

If the one you love is physically or verbally abusive, if he doesn't seem to care about your feelings, or if he does things such as comparing you unfavorably with past lovers, then there's no reason to proceed with the relationship. Anyone who would do such things in a dating relationship is going to be pure hell in a marriage.

A Word about Men

Before signing off, I need to say a quick word especially to the ladies. So, guys . . . please excuse us for a moment, will you?

Thanks.

Okay, ladies, I want to give you a little bit of advice about men.

I can't tell you how many times I've counseled women who told me that their lovers changed completely once they became husbands instead of boyfriends.

What do they mean by that?

Well:

"He spends every weekend glued to the football games on TV. I feel like football comes first and me second with him."

Or "The man is insatiable when it comes to sex. He never gives me a rest!"

Well, the truth is that men and women communicate in different ways. A woman who is aware of these differences will pick up on certain signals early in the relationship that will save her a great deal of trouble and confusion later on.

Actually, very early on in the relationship, any man will tell you what he's all about.

For instance, suppose you are dating a man who is divorced and you ask him what went wrong in his marriage.

"Oh, I don't know. Sex was great before marriage—but then once we got married it just wasn't so hot anymore."

He's told you right there that sex is on the front burner with him.

Or perhaps he tells you that he's got season tickets to the local football team.

That translates out to "Sports are very important in my life." And if it's tickets, plural, he could also be saying, "And I expect sports to be important in your life too."

All I am saying here, ladies, is that you need to learn how to understand the meaning that lies behind what your lover says to you.

Do that and you won't have some unpleasant surprises regarding his personality and character once you've been to the altar.

Okay, guys, you can come back in now.

Love Is . . .

How do you know if you're really in love? There's an ancient book that contains a description of love. The book is nearly two thousand years old, but it is still the best description of love I've ever read. There could be no finer words to use in closing our discussion about love and marriage. The book is the Bible—and from First Corinthians, chapter thirteen, we read:

"Love is patient, love is kind. It does not envy, it does not boast, it is not proud. It is not rude, it is not self-seeking, it is not easily angered, it keeps no record of wrongs. Love does not delight in evil but rejoices with the truth. It always protects, always trusts, always hopes, always perseveres.

"Love never fails."

Is It Love—or a Bad
Case of Heartburn?
(A test designed to help you know the difference)

Are the following statements true or false?

1. When I am not with the one I love I can't concentrate on anything else but how much I miss him.
2. Whenever I see my lover talking to another member of my sex, I get so jealous, I can't stand it.
3. I honestly don't think I could function without the one I love. If he ever left me, I know I'd die.
4. I honestly don't think the one I love could function without me, and if I ever left, he would probably die.
5. Sometimes I don't like my love very much, but he has such a hold over me that I just can't help myself.
6. My lover and I never seem to talk about anything except how much we love each other.
7. My lover is perfect, and I wouldn't change a single thing about him.
8. My lover is far from perfect, but I know I'll be able to change him once we're married.
9. My lover tends to make jokes at my expense, but it's okay because I know he's only teasing.
10. I don't care about my own happiness, but I'll do anything to make my lover happy.

The "false" answer was best in all of these questions, and here's why:

1. If you can't think about anything but your lover when you're not with him, it's infatuation and not love. Love may grow from infatuation, but it is not so full of anxiety and single-mindedness.
2. The same is true here. If you are insanely jealous of your lover, or if he is insanely jealous of you, there's something

not quite right about the relationship. Love must include a great deal of a thing called "trust."

3 and 4. Love is not emotional dependence, either your dependence upon someone else, or his dependence upon you.

5. If you can't control yourself, take a step back and ask yourself, "If I could control myself, would I choose to fall in love with this person?" If not, you're heading in the wrong direction.

6. Life is not all love-talk and romance. Are you comfortable making small-talk with your lover or talking about world affairs? If not, how do you know if you really have anything in common?

7. If you really think your lover is perfect, you'd better take another look at him, because nobody's *really* perfect.

8. If your lover does things that worry you now, while you're dating, what makes you think he'll change once you've married him? Chances are he'll become even worse. After all, he'll be letting his guard down once he's caught you!

9. If your lover makes jokes at your expense—even innocent, rather harmless jokes—it's a sign of either meanness, or that he's not as considerate of your feelings as he ought to be. Either way it's a bad sign.

10. It's unhealthy not to care about yourself. You can put your lover first, but your feelings had better matter to you too. If you don't think you're important enough to worry about your own happiness, you could be heading for an extremely one-sided relationship.

Now, don't think that a "true" answer on any of these questions is a sign that your relationship is doomed. But if you answer "true" on three or more of them, it's time to reassess the situation.

NOTES

CHAPTER ONE

1. Lucille Forer, *The Birth Order Factor* (New York: David McKay Co., Inc., 1976), p. 11.
2. Donald J. Trump with Tony Schwartz, *Trump: The Art of the Deal* (New York: Random House, 1987), p. 50.

CHAPTER THREE

1. Walter Toman, *Family Constellation* (New York: Springer Publishing Company, Inc., 1976).
2. Forer, op. cit. pp. 187–188.
3. Pamela Withers, "What Birth Order Says About Some Famous Romances," *Cosmopolitan,* September 1986.

CHAPTER FOUR

1. Dr. Alfred Adler, *The Practice of Individual Psychology* (London: K. Paul, Trench, Trubner & Co., Ltd, 1924), p. 3.
2. "A Special Kind of Love," article in *USA Today,* December 23, 1986.

CHAPTER FIVE

1. Gay Norton Edelman, "Why Can't We Talk to Each Other?" *Redbook,* April 1986.

CHAPTER SIX

1. Bradford Wilson and George Edington, *First Child, Second Child* (New York: McGraw-Hill Book Co., 1981), p. 92.

CHAPTER SEVEN

1. Jeanette Lauer and Robert Lauer, "Marriages Made to Last," *Psychology Today,* June 1985.

CHAPTER NINE

1. Walter Toman, op. cit. p. 76.

Index

M

older sister with female
Later-Born Middle, 129
personality traits of, 16–19, 23,
111–12, 132, 133, 135–46,
150, 152
within a relationship, 158–64
dealing with finances, 160
dealing with stress, 162–63
during leisure time, 159–60
parenting, 162
religion and philosophy, 163–
64
sexual relationship, 161
social relationships, 160–61
at work, 159
relationship between two
Middle Borns, 14
communication, 118–26
compromise, 112–15, 117–18,
132
pent-up feelings, 114–16, 118
sexual relationship, 122–23
as romantic detective, 147–65
traits to look for in a mate,
150–57
being sure the relationship is
something the Middle
Child wants, 152–54
reliability, faithfulness, and
honesty, 150–52
mutual respect, 154–57
various types of, 126–27
well known, 18, 19, 132
Mistakes, ability to laugh at your,
57, 75
Money, marrying for, 91–92
see also Finances, dealing with
Monogamy:
Middle Borns and, 19, 133
reasons for long-lasting
marriages, 164–65
Montana, Joe, 12
Moodiness, 56
Mother:
don't look for a woman who is

going to baby you like
your, 93–96
don't marry someone because
she doesn't remind you of
your, 82–86
don't marry someone because
you're reminded of your,
79–82
see also Father; Opposite-sex
family members; Parenting
Murphy, Eddie, 24

N

Neatness, 216
Negotiators, Middle Borns as, 16,
19, 132, 133
"working things out," 157–58
Nixon, Richard, 18
Nurturing:
need for, 192
need to nurture, 192

O

Officer and a Gentleman, An, 99
O'Neal, Tatum, 76
Only Child, 9–12
best match for, 11
myths about, 9–10
personality traits of, 10–12
well known, 10, 12
worst match for, 11, 30
see also Firstborns
Opposite-sex family members:
don't look for someone who
isn't at all like mommy or
daddy, 82–86
don't look for someone who
reminds you of mommy or
daddy, 79–82
importance of, 67–68, 93, 138
of Middle Borns, 127
Organizational skills:
of Firstborns, 13, 56, 60, 61–62,
102–103, 208, 216
of Last Borns, 60, 208, 216

Look for Dr. Kevin Leman's other best-selling titles!

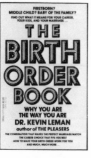

THE BIRTH ORDER BOOK
Why You Are the Way You Are

Your birth order—whether you were born first, second, or later in your family— powerfully influences what kind of person you are, whom you marry, the job you choose, and the kind of parent you'll be. Dr. Leman reveals an exciting new way to better understand yourself and those you love—through birth order.

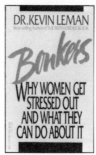

BONKERS
Why Women Get Stressed Out and What They Can Do About It

Are you burned out? Washed up? At the end of your rope? Here's a life raft for any woman drowning in an ocean of stress. Discover how to beat the Superwoman Syndrome; survive the stress of single parenthood; cope with two careers—in the office and at home; and much more.

MEASURING UP
How to Break the Cycle of Failure and Rejection and Become a Winner at Last!

Uncover the secrets to strong self-esteem. On the job, as a parent, as a spouse, learn how to succeed and discover the keys to happiness.

THE PLEASERS
Women Who Can't Say No— and the Men Who Control Them

Are you "yessing" your life away? Learn how to move from no power to No! power! Take charge of your life.

Dell

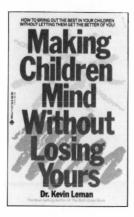